F. F. PROCTOR
VAUDEVILLE PIONEER

BY

WILLIAM MOULTON MARSTON

AND

JOHN HENRY FELLER

William Moulton Marston

William Moulton Marston was born on 9 May, 1893 in Cliftondale, Massachusetts, USA. He is known for accomplishments as diverse as psychologist, inventor, comic book creator and feminist theorist. Marston received his early education at Harvard University, graduating with B.A. in 1915, L.L.B. in 1918, and Ph.D. in Psychology in 1921, immediately moving to Washington D.C. to embark on a teaching career at *American University*, followed by *Tufts University* in Medford, MA. During his time at these universities, Marston produced several influential psychological theories regarding gender, emotions and their relationship with blood pressure. He is credited with the invention of the *Systolic Blood Pressure* test although it has been stated that Marston's wife, Elizabeth Holloway Marston should have been cited as a collaborator, with many scholars referring to Elizabeth's work on her husband's research. From his psychological work,

Marston was convinced that women were able to work quicker and more precisely, also being more truthful and dependable. He penned these observations in the *Emotions of Normal People* (1928), which argued that individuals act along two axes, with their responsiveness being either passive or active dependant relative to their perception of his or her environs as favourable or antagonistic. Marston posited that masculine notions of freedom are inherently anarchic and violent (linked to activity), opposed to feminine notions of 'Love Allure' that leads to 'an ideal state of submission to loving authority.' In addition to such theorising, Marston's most famous achievement is the creation of the *Wonder Woman* comic book character, inspired by his wife Elizabeth as well as his former student Olive Byrne, who lived with the couple in a polyamorous relationship. In the early 1940s, Marston wanted to create a feminine superhero to counteract the male dominated DC Comics Line. She was to be the model of a conventional yet powerful modern woman; 'tender, submissive, peace-loving as good women are', combining 'all the strength of a superman plus all the allure of a good and beautiful woman.' His character had superhuman strength and agility, as well as a magic lasso which forced villains to tell the truth when bound by it. Themes of bondage and submission in *Wonder Woman* reflected Marston's controversial 'sex love training' theory, whereby people can be trained to embrace compliance through eroticism. Except for four months in 2006, the series has been in print ever since its debut in 1941. Marston died of Cancer on May 2, 1947 in Rye, New York. He was entered into the Comic Book Hall of Fame in 2006.

Contents

		PAGE
	Top Billing	11
	Program Note	13
	An Acknowledgment to a Host of Contributors	14
	A Letter from Mr. George M. Cohan	15

CHAPTER		
I	Enter: Freddie Proctor	17
II	The Great Levantine	33
III	King of Vaudeville	45
IV	Building the Big Time	72
V	Double Harness	96
VI	A Sterling Helpmate	119
VII	Ring Down the Curtain	143
VIII	Monuments to the Man	158

Pictures

Fred Levantine, Equilibrist of the '70s
The Tremont Gymnasium
An F. F. Levantine Poster of the '70s
Three Rare Tintypes: Levantine Brothers, Georgie Mills at 12 and at 16
Levantine's Billing at Tony Pastor's
Jerry Cohan and Frederick F. Levantine
Proctor as an Acrobat, from *New York Dramatic Mirror*, January 30, 1909
An early Levantine Billing

[*Between pages* 32–33]

Fred Proctor at 18
F. F. Proctor at 21 (in 1872)
Mr. Proctor in His Prime
F. F. Proctor in 1905
Mr. Proctor at Miami in 1924
Mr. and Mrs. Proctor on Their Central Valley Estate
Mr. Proctor's last Photograph
George E. and Clarence H. Wallen

[*Between pages* 48–49]

New Bowery Theatre Program
Olympia Theatre Program
Georgie Lingard's first Billing
First Proctor (Levantine) Program
Proctor's 25th Anniversary Jubilee
New Bowery Theatre Program

[*Between pages* 64–65]

Sir Harry Lauder
The Four Cohans
George M. Cohan
Lillian Russell Handbill
Lillian Russell
New York Theatre Managers
New York Theatre Proprietors
Nellie Lingard

[*Between pages* 80–81]

A Triple Program, 1889
Proctor's Theatre Programs, 1894
Proctor House Advertisements, 1894
Georgie Lingard Billed at Proctor's Fifth Avenue Theatre, 1902
Night Picture of Proctor's Newark Theatre, 1906
Newspaper Clippings

[*Between pages* 96–97]

Georgena Lingard with Skipping Rope
Georgie Lingard, Champion Skipping-rope Dancer
Georgie Lingard in the Days of Her Bowery Triumphs
Georgie Lingard in Dance on Darkened Stage
Georgie Lingard in Character Roles
Georgie Lingard in Three Early Roles: "The Essence of Old Virginia," "Little Lord Fauntleroy," the "Flower Girl" Act
Georgie Lingard as Daffy in "Mrs. B. O'Shaughnessy"
Georgie Lingard's Little Lost Girl Act

[*Between pages* 128–129]

☆

Georgie Lingard in Her Teens
Georgie Lingard in 1876 and 1877
Georgie Lingard at 21 (in 1882)

Portrait of Georgie Taken for Her Mother
Mrs. F. F. Proctor (Georgena Mills)
Mrs. Proctor Soon after her Marriage
Mrs. Proctor Celebrating her Eightieth Birthday
Mrs. Proctor in 1942
       [*Between pages* 144–145]

Mr. Proctor's Coat of Arms
Parents of Mr. and Mrs. Proctor
Proctoria, at Central Valley, N. Y.
The Proctor Yachts, "Georgena I" and "Georgena II"
Georgie Lingard on Elephant in the Forepaugh Parade
An Audience at Proctor's Pleasure Palace, 1899
Obituaries
Proctor's 23rd Street Theatre
      [*Between pages* 160–161]

Top Billing

It is a privilege and a pleasant task to record the story of a long life, a rich life, a life full of good works, the career of Frederick Freeman Proctor, dean of American vaudeville managers and maker of theatrical history.

We have all too many instances of success achieved by those who rode rough-shod over everything and everybody in their path of ambition—and all too few inspiring records of lives which spread goodness and happiness in all their contacts, achieving greatness without taking unfair advantage of their fellow humans.

One of the most outstanding of these rare stories, the life and work of F. F. Proctor, has never been adequately told because Mr. Proctor shunned personal publicity, preferring to do his good deeds for their own sake.

To assist in this work, those who loved and respected him through his long life and his very successful business career have undertaken this affectionate monument to his memory.

This book sticks to the record and its pages are free from overstatement, because he would want it that way.

The story of this exemplary character in American business is a balm to jittery nerves in today's hectic world. The gratifying portrait of Mr. Proctor's live-and-let-live personality makes his personal history at once an inspiration and a beaconlight of faith in the simple, good life.

As a heritage to posterity, this story of the life of F. F. Proctor—whose name and career represent a landmark in theatrical affairs in the East—is issued with the special blessing of Mrs. Georgena Mills Proctor, his helpmate for more than a quarter of a century.

WILLIAM MOULTON MARSTON

Rye, New York.
September, 1943

Program Note

This is the story of a man who saved his own soul because he did not want to gain the whole world.

There may have been in his time a combination of men that owned a slightly larger theatre circuit or controlled a vaster corporation than Mr. F. F. Proctor, but he was a king in his own right.

The story of his life has many lessons for those who would make their mark in the entertainment field. It demonstrates that business success and decency are not incompatible. Mr. Proctor was loyal to his employees and let them have a substantial share in his success. Thus he gave living proof of the noble potentialities of the American Way.

JOHN HENRY FELLER

AN ACKNOWLEDGMENT TO A HOST OF CONTRIBUTORS

Assembling material for this biography was made easy by contemporary historians of the theatre and by the editors, reporters and feature writers of newspapers and of special publications who faithfully reported Mr. Proctor's achievements. His personality was impressed upon the hearts and minds of all who came into contact with him during his long and constructive life. So the material for this book was ready at hand upon consulting the newspaper archives and upon inviting those who knew Mr. Proctor to submit their recollections, anecdotes, pictures and mementos.

A newspaper man of twenty years' metropolitan experience testifies to the inherent value of the press record of Mr. Proctor's many activities, for he found not one clipping that could have resulted from a self-seeking impulse or high-pressure publicity.

The Harvard University Theatre Collection, the Theatre Section of the New York Public Library and the Davis Collection, were valuable sources of data and pictures.

The authors express their thanks to every publication, organization and individual cited or quoted in these pages.

W.M.M. & J.H.F.

A LETTER FROM MR. GEORGE M. COHAN

George M. Cohan
152 West 42nd Street
New York

March 28, 1942

Dear Mrs. Proctor—

It was good to hear from you. I am so glad you are doing Mr. Proctor's biography. It will I am sure be most interesting. I wish I could add something worthwhile to the story of *The Great Little Man,* as my Dad always called him, but alas I'm afraid I am not capable of doing a very good job along such lines.

I can however tell you this. From the time I was a kid I remember how proud my Dad was of the Proctor success and how he related to me the story of Mr. Proctor's rise from circus performer to one of the most influential and successful theatre managers of America. Of course my Dad was a sentimentalist of the first order. Being Irish, he naturally was very emotional and used to tell the Proctor story with great pride and a tear in his voice at the same time.

Then, too, of course later on in life when we played for Mr. Proctor at the old 23rd St. Theatre, I can remember his visits to our dressing room and the warmth of his greeting to our family and the great joy he and Dad seemed to get out of their talks of the *good old days.*

Then, later on again, when we first went to live in Orange County and we became neighbors, I can recall the happy visits to the Proctor home and the Proctor visits to the Cohan home. It was a real education to me to listen to Mr. Proctor and my Dad going back over the years and living again so to speak through their early experiences in the Theatre World. I said to my Dad one day, "It must have been wonderful, the great friendship that existed between the performers of early days." He replied, "Son, it was more than friendship, it was a real brotherhood." And I guess it must have been, the way they seemed to enjoy one another's success.

Naturally, Mr. Proctor was the great favorite of all the variety performers. And of course the reason for that was because of the fact that he himself had at one time been one of the rank and file and had served his apprenticeship and had come up the hard way.

And then again, I myself have had something to feel very proud about as far as the rise of The Proctors is concerned. I had the great honor of playing on the same bill with Mrs. Proctor some years before she became Mrs. Proctor. And what a fine performer and what a beautiful young woman she was! Oh, yes, I can remember it all as vividly as though it happened only yesterday.

Well, my dear, I guess that's about all I can say because there isn't much left to say except that without these fond memories life wouldn't mean very much. I do hope you are well and happy and I also hope that as you are working on the biography you'll let me know how it is going along. I can assure you, my dear, that I'll read it with great interest when it is finished and enjoy every word of it. God bless you and best love from Mrs. Cohan.

Sincerely,

GEORGE M.

P.S. I'm leaving for Monroe today. Do you ever go to Central Valley these days? It's beautiful up there this time of year as you know.

G. M. C.

ACT ONE

Enter Freddie Proctor

Overhead the Maine sky had depths of blue that seemed an appropriate arch for the healthful world an eight-year-old boy knew at the end of the eighteen-fifties. He was on his way home from school. The great pine forests rose in splendor about him. The mighty ocean, beating against the shores he trod, built up the soul and heart of this Maine lad. These forests and this ocean seem to have purified and held in treasure the Maine air and sunshine especially for his lungs.

In time the strong will and stout limbs of this little Maine lad, whose sturdy ancestors had come over in the Mayflower, were to carry him into foreign lands, before crowned heads in capitals of Europe, under northern skies even bleaker than those of Maine, and under the warmer blues of the sunlit Mediterranean heavens.

In the years to come his strong limbs were to carry him into possession of great means, ease and comfort, and his hands, already strong on his homemade trapeze, would hold the reins of the Proctor theatrical empire. But the great qualities that characterize Maine and Maine men remained with him, even when his career took him far from the Pine Tree State. Throughout his life he remained, in sterling simplicity, integrity and idealism, the Maine boy who was returning from school that afternoon and going directly to the cellar of his home.

In that year 1859, the Civil War was brewing, but the greatest interest in his life was that boulder-walled room. His heart quickened as he descended the stairs and his nostrils snuffed eagerly the earthiness that clung in the delightful coolness of Dr. Alpheus Proctor's cellar. Dr. Proctor was the country physician of the town of Dexter, Maine. Here he lived with his wife, the former Lucy Ann Tufts, and their five children. In later years his son was to remember pleasantly the place of his birth, particularly the basement he had converted into a boy's gymnasium, and to reckon it a foundation for his entire life.

A well-worn tumbling mat covered the floor. Overhead hung a trapeze. Standing on end near the cellar wall was a small barrel with ends nailed up and sides beaten smooth by many midair performances at the tips of the youngster's toes. In another corner were other devices the boy had seen in traveling shows and carnivals and had made the best he could from memory.

Young Proctor had haunted every itinerant show that passed through his town. Something far too big even for his well-developed frame seemed to yearn and stretch within him when he saw the troupes of the time unfolding their tents, spreading out the spangles they had carried over tedious trails once beaten by Indians, and readying themselves for the shows they gave. They were a hard-bitten lot, the men sinewy, rugged and always poised ready for emergency, and the women taut and daring, with a feline, slender grace and eyes filled with a worldly wisdom that takes the trials and triumphs of life in easy stride.

Young Proctor in his cellar would reach easily for his trapeze and draw himself upward, imitating the barnstorming acrobat who had thrilled the farmers and village folks the week before. The trying routine was not so hard, for he remembered the shouting crowds, the troupers' indifference to danger and the romance of it all! Did not he recall watching some sideshow folding up in the moonlight after the performance, the band music still vibrant in the night? Could not he almost feel the starlight creeping down into the space abandoned by the departing show's lanterns?

There wasn't much more than that to tempt this boy. The

show business was hazardous and seemed to offer little for those interested mainly in financial gain.

In 1851, the year Freddie Proctor was born, Stephen C. Foster gave the world "Old Folks At Home." Six years earlier Foster had written a song that was such a favorite in the Proctor household that Freddie could remember all the words years later in the eighteen-nineties when he was discussing Foster with one of his stage managers:

UNCLE NED

There was an old darky;
His name was Uncle Ned;
He died long years ago.
He had no hair on the top of his head,
In the place where the wool ought to grow.

Chorus

Lay down the shovel and the hoe;
Pick up the fiddle and the bow.
There's no mo' work for poor Uncle Ned,
'Cause he's gone where de good darkies go.

Almost every week, musical soirees were held in the Proctor living room, and the children listened spell-bound to spirited vocalizations by the near-great and plain home-grown baritones and sopranos and hard-to-classify singers who gathered around the piano. The walls would vibrate to the strains of the old favorite "Rocked in the Cradle of the Deep" (written in 1831), the Stephen Foster masterpieces and such martial airs of the war between the states as Julia Ward Howe's "Battle Hymn of the Republic," sung to the tune of "John Brown's Body"; George F. Root's "Battle Cry of Freedom" and "Tramp, Tramp, Tramp, the Boys Are Marching"; and Henry Clay Work's "Marching Through Georgia."

Negro minstrelsy, which began in the eighteen-forties, was at its height in young Proctor's boyhood. "Boston was the place of origin for more burnt cork shows than the rest of the country combined," says M. B. Leavitt in his *Fifty Years in Theatrical Management* (1912), and the minstrel shows were popular in New England before any other part of the country—so we may be sure that young Proctor in Maine was acquainted with this thoroughly American form of entertainment which combined music, sentiment, dancing, humor and tall tales. It is well to remember that such great legitimate actors as the Booths and Jo Jefferson got their stage start (Jefferson's at the age of four 'jumping Jim Crow') in blackface; that Dan Emmett's "Dixie" originated as a minstrel-show walk-around; that Foster's most famous songs were written for minstrels and were made popular by traveling troupes all over the country; and that Charley White's variety show, combining minstrel acts, specialties and burlesque, was the link between the blackface of Proctor's boyhood and the kind of entertainment he developed.

It was neither music nor minstrelsy that was young Freddie Proctor's main interest—but juggling and acrobatics. As he lay on his back, kicking a barrel until, spinning and bobbing faster and faster, it made the air fairly hum, he would image himself in a perfected version of his act, surpassing all other performers. These dreams he confided to his father and mother. They were not show people, and they could not quite understand his avid liking for the show business. His own insatiable curiosity about show folks had brought him the discouraging knowledge that the best performers were sons and daughters of performers.

After a year of persistent efforts to lay the groundwork for his career, what seemed to be a still greater discouragement came to him. His father was stricken in 1860 and died that year. Freddie was only nine years old when his mother was left a widow with five young children. Not yet in his teens, he had to leave school and take on the responsibilities of life, and this very circumstance in life gave his ambition another push.

His mother was of hardened New England fiber, and she met emergencies bravely. She packed up her belongings and took her children back to the Tufts ancestral farm at Lexington, Massachusetts. Friendly neighbors welcomed them, and Freddie was shown the places where his father had courted his mother and the farm his grandfather had worked as a lad. He took readily to farm work, his chores were easy for him, and he was rapidly learning a good deal about life. He was proud in later years to remember that his mother had come from Lexington and that her great-grandfather had died in the battle fought there in April of 1775. He knew the exact spot where the old hero had died. His father's family came from Concord,* where the embattled farmers first struck for freedom.

Freddie Proctor had his own way to make. He soon left Lexington for Boston. His first job there was with a millinery firm, wrapping packages all day, delivering them after the store closed, and getting a dollar a week. Within a few weeks, he found a better position with Browning & Jenkins, a drygoods house that was soon bought by two of the employees and became R. H. White & Company, the largest drygoods firm in Boston.

---

* From the January 1931 issue of *The New England Historical and Genealogical Register*, published by the New England Historic Genealogical Society, Boston:

"Frederick Freeman Proctor, of Larchmont, N. Y., elected a Pilgrim Tercentenary member 3 December 1919, was born at Dexter, Me., 17 March 1851, the son of Alpheus and Lucy Ann (Tufts) Proctor, and died at Larchmont 4 September 1929.

"He was a descendant of Robert [1] Proctor a freeman of Concord, Mass., in 1643 and later, in 1654, a settler at Chelmsford, Mass., where he died in 1697, whose wife was Jane Hildreth, through Peter,[2] 1652–1730, who married Mary Patterson, Peter,[3] 1694–1772, who married Hannah Harwood Simeon,[4] 1729–1820, whose wife was Rebecca Foster, Simeon [5] of Littleton, Mass., who was born in 1760 and married Charlotte Hudson, and Alpheus,[6] his father, a physician at Sangerville, Bangor, Dexter, and other towns in Maine, who was born at Littleton 27 January 1806 and married in April 1835 Lucy Ann Tufts (born at Lexington, Mass., 11 July 1811, the daughter of Thomas and Rebecca (Adams) Tufts)."

Freddie's income jumped to six dollars a month, and he worked his way from cash boy to bundle boy, wrapping packages all day and delivering them at night.

Hard work was agreeable to his muscular frame. The rudiments of business captured his respect for good order, and his later business success owed much to R. H. White's store where he learned to think of management as a necessary part of all enterprise.

As he worked away behind a small partition, he could hear the talk of customers in the store. Boston then in its own opinion was the center of the universe, or at least the cultural capital of America. He heard tales of the progress of the theatre. He heard some of his own great heroes laughed at as backwoods provincials, for some folks in Boston did not realize that Horace Greeley was the greatest man who ever lived, though back in Maine no farmer or townsman ever made a decision without looking in *The Weekly Tribune* to see what Greeley had to say on the subject. He heard of the theatre and one day a clerk in the store said to him:

"Listen, Freddie, if you really want to see an acrobatic show, go without dinner sometime and take in the Hanlon Brothers."

That night Freddie passed a few coins through a ticket office window and climbed the stairs to the balcony. It was an impressive show. High up in the dark crowd the little boy who was seeing the show at great personal sacrifice strained forward in his seat. The mold for his theatrical career was being cast.

The Hanlon Brothers, George, Alfred, Frederick and Edward, were from England, and they were famous. In January 1862, we learn from Tompkins' *History of the Boston Theatre*, "The Cataract of the Ganges" was presented at Goodwin and Wilder's Circus, with the Hanlon Brothers as an added attraction, featuring William Hanlon in *Zampillaerostation*, a word coined by James W. Lingard, manager of the Bowery Theatre, New York, for a trapeze act with no safety net.

ENTER FREDDIE PROCTOR

After witnessing the Hanlon Brothers in *Zampillaerostation,* Freddie Proctor put R. H. White's efforts to serve Boston in a second place in his life. In the basement of the store, he discovered a couple of packing boxes and a small barrel that he juggled now and then when he was alone. Each noon he carried his sandwich to the basement with him.

First, munching slowly, he would appraise the beams and the possibilities of a trapeze, and look for a clear space to do a little tumbling. Then, his sandwich gone, he spread out a few gunny sacks, lay on his back, and tried a medium-sized crate used for packing table cloths. It was a dangerous feat, for the wooden box might suddenly descend on him with the devastating effect of a wooden guillotine. The superintendent of the building, making his rounds from the other end of the basement, could not see the youngster lying on his back, as the rows of packing cases obscured the view, but he could see a linen crate bobbing around rapidly in midair. Curious to know what was going on, he edged closer and observed the bundle boy juggling a barrel and negotiating several other acrobatic stunts. The superintendent shook his head slowly and admiringly. "What are you doing?" he asked. "I've seen juggling, but I've never seen such good juggling. What else can you do?"

"Why I can tumble a little, and swing on a trapeze."

"Trapeze—of course," said the superintendent. "That's just what I need—exercise on a trapeze. Say, Freddie, I've got just the kind of rope we need. Listen. Come here tomorrow at noontime and we'll have a first-rate trapeze. Now skadoodle. Your lunch hour is up, and if you don't get back to your wrapping, I'll report you for loafing." And he gave the youngster a friendly slap on the back to show him that he liked him.

The trapeze in White's basement was a tremendous success. To Freddie's consternation, for a time several other employees wanted to exercise there at lunchtime, but it was only a passing fancy for all but Freddie, and he soon was able to have the trapeze to himself for about twenty-five minutes every noon. In the other five minutes of the lunch period he ate his sandwich. At other times in the day he would find excuses to go to the basement. He seemed always to be running out of string or paper. On each trip downstairs he'd get in at least a few turns on the trapeze.

His skill won the admiration of all the boys in the store, and he became a leader in their gymnastics. When the weather was good, he led the youngsters to the green lawns of Boston Common, chose a thick grassy spot, and taught them the pyramids. They were soon organized into a skillful troupe, and had an appreciative audience awaiting them each noon.

Young Freddie's addiction to the trapeze impressed the members of White's management with his skill, but persuaded them that he wasn't contributing much to their efforts as Boston's leading merchants.

"Freddie would rather turn over a trapeze than do anything in the store," the head secretary remarked.

"He's a likable lad, but maybe he would be happier elsewhere," one of the managers said. "I hoped if he kept his nose to the grindstone he would soon be one of our best salesmen."

So it was decided that young Freddie Proctor's stay with White's had better be ended. This was a blessing in disguise for him and for the American theatre, for he was saved from the life of a merchant.

His married sister, Louisa Tufts Cummings, twenty years his senior, persuaded him to go back to school. He tried it, but after two months he decided he ought to be earning his own living and building a career.

The only memento he kept of these boyhood days was a letter he wrote to his mother when he was thirteen. It gives an inkling of the Yankee thrift in his character, and it exemplifies the brevity of his correspondence throughout his life. In a neat hand, he wrote:

ENTER FREDDIE PROCTOR

March 21st, 1864.

DEAR MOTHER:

I suppose you think it is strange why I have not written before, but to tell the truth, I have not had time. My school is over and has been about two weeks. Uncle Bowen went to the examination. Noney is out of school now. I heard that Eler had been sick with some kind of fever. I am very sorry. I have got to get me a new cap. Do you think I had better send this pattern and let you send it up, or shall I come and get it when I come down to spend the Sunday? Does Alphey's rubber boots turn out too small or not. I am sorry if they did, for it would almost be the same as if he had lost three dollars. That is all I can write now. So good bye. Give my love to all the folks. Write soon.

* * *

He didn't bother to sign it when he wrote it, but, forty years later, attesting the sentimental value he attached to this early missive, he added the inscription: "From Fred F. Proctor. I signed this at 53; was thirteen when originally written." His mother died in August 1893 at Windsor, New Hampshire.

In later years, shortly after the turn of the century, he invariably signed his love letters to Georgie Lingard, "As ever, F. F. Proctor." When Georgie asked him, "Is that a way to sign a love letter?" he pleaded "But, dear, that's my style—I never sign my name any other way."

With his school days ended, he wandered up one tortuous Boston street and down another. He made careful note of all the theatres and especially the gymnasiums. While he had been at R. H. White's his shows on Boston Common had drawn several managers and circus agents to look over his group of performers. Some of them had offered Freddie a chance to enter a theatrical career, but when he learned that they wanted only him and not his entire troupe, he turned down their offers. Later this same sense of fairness won him a sterling reputation as an employer.

One of the agents who saw his act gave him the address of

the Tremont Club gymnasium and suggested that if he ever changed his mind he should come there to see him. Now Freddie joined this Tremont Gymnasium, which trained professional performers from all parts of the country to supply the ever-increasing number of traveling shows and circuses.

Freddie could not have dreamed of a better place. This gymnasium had professionally designed equipment, the very finest Indian clubs, dumbbells, cannon balls, etc. In the center of the gymnasium the instructors were helping the various students, men of all ages exercising with an avidness that stirred young Proctor. There was much lifting and heavy work with dumbbells weighing as much as a hundred and five pounds, forty-pound Indian clubs and cannon balls from eighteen to fifty pounds apiece. Every kind of trapeze was represented—there were flying rings, and single and double trapezes. Professor Du Crowe, the chief instructor, had been a slack-wire specialist with circuses in all parts of the country, and nearly all the feats he taught were for circus display.

Freddie tried out most of the apparatus, got a thorough warming up and then sat near the lockers watching the other performers. A sweaty athlete asked him: "Aren't you the chap who used to give performances with the gang on Boston Common?" When Freddie said "Yes," he asked him, "When did you join here?" Freddie replied, "I haven't joined yet, but that's what I came in for." Freddie was led over to Professor Du Crowe and introduced.

"You would like to join?" asked the instructor, admiring the boy's broad shoulders and strong wrists. "Remember our standards are high here. We are all professionals. We can't waste much time with beginners."

Young Fred suddenly sprang up and gripped a ring which had swung over his head. Pushing his legs forward, he increased his momentum in one swing enough to carry him in midair to a long-roped trapeze that was still in motion from the movements of another performer. Swinging himself high, he released one of his hands from the bar and swung in a large arc several times hanging by one arm. He ended the stunt by making a quick one-handed transfer back to the ring.

"Why didn't you say you are a professional and be done with it?" Du Crowe scolded. "Take off your shirt and begin anywhere," he commanded.

Where should he begin? He decided to go on the apparatus directly in front of him. When he had worked himself into a sweat, Du Crowe waved to him to quit and took him into his office. The application for membership was made out and Du Crowe, as he gave Freddie a hearty handshake, told him, "My boy, it's a great pleasure to enroll you. You're going to make good."

The Boston Y.M.C.A., which in 1872 took over the Tremont Club gymnasium, became famous for a training and body-building that was the direct opposite of the heavy work at the Tremont Club while it was a professional training place. Robert J. Roberts, superintendent of the Boston Y.M.C.A. gymnasium, advocated in the eighteen-seventies "safe, easy, short, beneficial and pleasing" exercise. But by the time Freddie Proctor heard of this mild form of training he was already well on the way toward becoming one of the most expert performers in New England. He was strictly a product of the "heavy work" school, for the Tremont Gymnasium had offered no other type of training.

At the Tremont Gymnasium he spent several weeks of intensive training. His guardian-angel sister Louise paid his tuition and living expenses. Then he won a place in Professor Du Crowe's Exhibition Class which gave weekly performances. One of these Saturday night shows brought him his first engagement.

A swarthy young spectator at one of these shows, who was about eighteen years old at the time and whose name no one knows—Leavitt thinks he was an Italian—walked over to Freddie after Du Crowe had finished showing off his star pupil and said: "I'm looking for an assistant to carry my equipment back and forth from the theatre wings, and maybe we can try some joint juggling."

Freddie jumped at the chance. "When do we start?" he cried out. "But I have no tights or . . ."

That night, the future King of Vaudeville trod the boards in the glare of the footlights of a Boston variety hall. He carried the Indian clubs and pyramids for the swarthy performer and worked with him in several juggling acts.

His boyish manner and his quiet skill brought him considerable applause. That first night together on the stage they made such a hit that the older partner decided to make the alliance permanent. Immediately after the show he told young Proctor:

"Fred, you have a new brother! From now on our act will be billed as 'The Levantine * Brothers.' It's a good stage name, and I've bought the rights to it from a retired team."

The first engagement of The Levantine Brothers was at the Theatre Comique in Boston, where they did nine turns a day and got $10 a week—supposedly $5 each, but Freddie saw very little of the ten dollars after the theatre manager paid it to his partner. This was particularly unfair, for the success of the team was due largely to the boyish charm, modesty and skill that Freddie Proctor contributed.

However, before many months rolled by, he got free from his exploiter. One day, while the two were rehearsing a new act in the Tremont Gymnasium, Freddie's partner whispered to him that M. B. Leavitt, the great theatrical manager, had just entered and was looking them over.

* The first Levantine on the American stage was an Italian. The word "Levantine" means "from the Levant," that is the eastern Mediterranean, and the swarthy athlete may have been a Greek or Armenian. But on the American stage the name was to be made famous by the down-east boy Fred Proctor.

Leavitt was instantly impressed, called Fred over, and said, "Very good juggling, lad! May I see your act?"

The other Levantine edged over. But Leavitt's attention was all for Fred Proctor. When Proctor explained to his new boss that many of his acts required a partner, Leavitt told him to find one who was better than his former associate.

Professor Du Crowe recommended George E. Mansfield, then twenty-two, who had run away from home five years before and joined a circus much to the dismay of his church-going family. Mansfield was a handsome chap, son of the owner of a Boston shoe store. The team soon received offers from other managers, and it was not long before they had a joint salary of a hundred dollars a week. They traveled with L. B. Lent's Circus for more than five years.

In the Brander Matthews Dramatic Museum of Columbia University the programs of the New York Circus, at 14th Street opposite the Academy of Music, L. B. Lent manager, show that the Levantine Brothers appeared there, together or singly, on the following dates:

    1866, Oct. 15—Feats on the Horizontal Bar
    1868, Mar. 13—Le Double Trapeze
      "   " 27—"   "   "
      "   Oct. 27—On the Horizantal Bar
      "   Nov. 10—Crystal Pyramids
    1869, Mar. 5—Crystal Pyramids and Magic Barrel

And in October 1869 they were with Lent's Circus at New Brighton.

The earliest "famous first" among Mr. Proctor's many novelties was the *jewelled barrel*. He realized that spectators, especially those farthest from the stage, could not tell whether a common barrel made one revolution or twenty as it was kicked up by the tumbler. How could he heighten the spectators' appreciation of the varied gyrations, the difficult twirlings, of the barrels, pyramids, chairs, tables and other objects that he juggled?

Spangling these objects with brightly colored paints did not give the effect he wanted. He finally took a barrel and inlaid it with pieces of glass, some brightly colored and some with mirrors of silver or gold. The effect was dazzling, like giant rubies and emeralds. Modern-day electric flicker signs are no more dazzling than the "gem-encrusted" barrels described and pictured in old lithographs and posters of the Fred Levantine acts.

Fred and George received many offers, and the proposition that separated them illustrates the characters of the partners.

George announced, "Fred, I'm going to Europe! I've got an offer!"

Proctor asked dubiously, "Europe?"

"Yes, Fred," shot back George, "And I'm wild about it. Europe at my age—why that would be hitting the top and we're only beginning!"

Fred Proctor shook his head. No, he wasn't excited—he seldom lost his calm, then or later in his career. Naturally George Mansfield was exasperated.

"All of Europe!" exclaimed Mansfield. "Just think! I'm going before people of all cultures. I'll see the Danube, the gaiety of Vienna, the spires of St. Petersburg. Imagine playing before kings and queens!" Soon Proctor was hearing glowing reports of George's success in the strange lands, and before a year had rolled around, George was trying to convince Freddie that he ought to join him. And then Freddie himself received an attractive offer for a European tour which he accepted.

* * *

In 1872, just before embarking on his first trip to Europe, Mr. Proctor married Mary Ann Daily of New York, a singer and actress, who had made her debut at the age of thirteen, at

ENTER FREDDIE PROCTOR

the New Bowery Theatre, at a benefit for a Mrs. W. G. Jones, and later was a member of Kate Fisher's Dramatic Company. Her stage name was Polly Daily. She was popular in the early seventies, and Robert Grau called her "the very best seriocomic that the variety stage could boast of." She retired from the stage soon after Mr. Proctor opened his first theatre in Albany. Of their marriage were born Fred, Jr., who was later his father's assistant, and two daughters, Ellenor and Henrietta. She died on September 28, 1901 and, of the three children, only the daughters survived their father.

* * *

During the voyage to Europe and on his tour, Mr. Proctor was unobtrusively studying human nature, as if to make up for his all-too-short schooling. In Europe—as at home—he learned the ways of cosmopolitan people and the rules and possibilities of his own profession.

In Europe he was received with an acclaim beyond his fondest expectations. Yankee ingenuity had considerable to offer the crowned heads of Europe, and he had prepared himself to show Europe his best. At no time did he let his wits become dull, or stop his studies. He learned time and place utility. He learned the psychology of crowds, what an audience wanted and what he could give it. He learned how a successful trick in one field may be transferred to another. He stored up an enormous reservoir of ideas, features, novelties.

While Proctor was in Europe he occasionally saw his old partner George Mansfield. While walking along Unter den Linden in Berlin, Freddie remarked, "See, when people are shopping, or relaxing, they are ready for the theatre." That idea he later applied in New York. On another occasion, as they sat in a restaurant in Vienna, Fred said, "Just listen to that music," and he tucked away the idea that his theatrical enterprises of the future would have to have great musical numbers and the best orchestras available. "Music is a kind of mystical scenery," he thought.

He noticed the splendid quality of European variety shows. "Variety in America," he said, "is like a house that is good in design but is composed of cheap material. I'll build the house of variety with the best material to be had."

After three years abroad, Proctor decided to return to America.*

Immediately upon his return from Europe, Proctor toured America for a year. Then in 1876 he made another European tour, reappearing at all the leading music halls he had played on the previous trip. Dan Bushnell was his new team-mate, and, to quote an old clipping, "In 1876, F. F. Levantine [Proctor] and Dan Bushnell sailed for America on the Steamship *Servia* from Copenhagen, Denmark, by way of Hamburg, after they had very successfully filled a series of engagements in Germany and most of the European countries."

Now he was intent on putting in practice the knowledge and experience he had gained abroad. American vaudeville, then slapstick, crude, provincial and generally revolting to finer tastes, was to become, by his efforts, cosmopolitan and acceptable to family groups.

(END OF ACT I)

* Mansfield continued successfully on his own in various countries of Europe for an additional ten years. Then, although still young, he lost his health and had to give up the stage. He entered the real estate business in Boston and acquired considerable business property there. Since Proctor wanted a playhouse in Boston, he proposed another partnership with his friend and jointly they opened the Grand Opera House on Washington Street in 1886. At the end of five years, this partnership was dissolved when Mansfield's failing health forced him to retire to private life. In 1906 he died of athletic heart.

Fred Levantine (Mr. Proctor), Equilibrist of the '70s

The Tremont Gymnasium where Mr. Proctor Developed His Acrobatic Skill

An F. F. Levantine Poster of the '70s

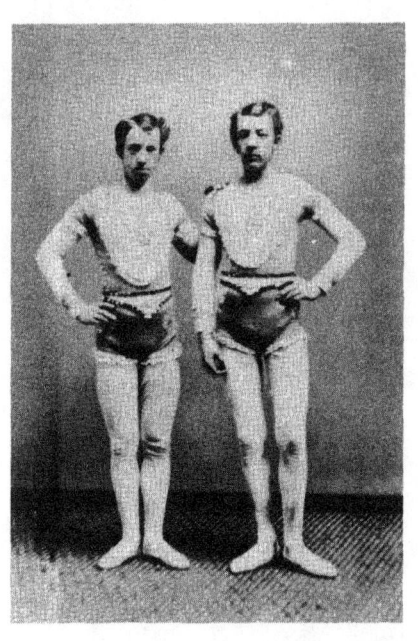

THREE RARE TINTYPES: LEVANTINE BROTHERS (PROCTOR, AT THE LEFT). GEORGIE MILLS AT 12 (ABOVE) AND 16 (LEFT) IN FIRST LONG DRESS

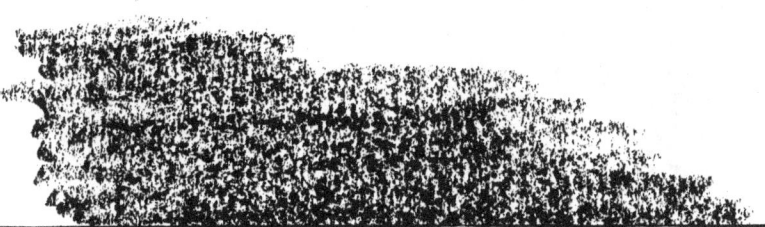

FRED LEVANTINE'S BILLING AT TONY PASTOR'S NEW THEATRE

FREDERICK F. LE'ZANTINE
EQUILIBRIST

IRISH COMIQUE.
1867.

PROCTOR AS AN ACROBAT.

Many are the leading men in the theatrical business world, as in other pursuits, who have started at the bottom of the ladder. In fact, nearly all have done so. There are also numerous managers who began their life work as actors or performers. Among the latter is F. F. Proctor.

Born at Dexter, Me., the son of a physician, he had the usual good schooling that comes to the son of prosperous parents. At an early age he went to Boston, where he joined the Young Men's Christian Association. In this organization he took every advantage of the gymnasium, and growing proficient in athletic work he joined hands with another young man and together they secured an engagement at a Boston theatre under the name of the Levantine Brothers. Their venture proved a big success, and for many years following the team toured the country, receiving it has been said, sometimes as much as $400 a week, which was an enormous salary for those times. Through the courtesy of J. Aldrich Libbey THE MIRROR herewith shows a picture of Mr. Proctor at this time, with another illustration advertising his act. As will be seen by these two illustrations, Mr. Proctor was working alone, having left his partner some time previous.

The success of Mr. Proctor as a vaudeville manager is too well known to require comment here, the object of this sketch being merely a reminder of the performing days of the distinguished manager rather than a résumé of his life.

FROM *New York Dramatic Mirror*, JANUARY 30, 1909

HARRY WOOD'S
NOVELTY THEATRE.

61 & 63 GREEN STREET.
Programme for this Evening.

The Evenings Entertainment will commence with the Laughable Farce

A QUIET FAMILY!

Barnaby Bibbs	NED WEST
Mrs. Barnaby Bibbs	Miss Minnie Wood
Johnathan Bibbs	Harry Wood
Mrs. Johnathan Bibbs	Miss Josie Crocker
OVERTURE	Orchestra

The Dashing Little Artiste
Miss LILLIE LAVERDE,

M'LLE SARBRO,
In Her Artistic Specialty
The Ladder of Life!
Walking on a Ladder of Sharp Edged Swords.

MISS POLLY DAILY
Pronounced by the Press and Public the Acme of the Novelty Stage.

FRED. F. LEVANTINE,
This Gentleman is the originator of his different acts, and the grace with which he performs his difficult feats is the theme of admiration and praise.
No. 1—Enchanted Globes.   No. 2—Table a la Mange.   No. 3—Magic Barrel.

OVERTURE, - - - - - Orchestra

First time of Ned West's Laughable Negro Farce, entitled
Don't Obstruct the Mail!

Jake—(Mail Carrier)	Mr. NED WEST
Charles—(a Lover)	Mr. Harry Wood
Fannie Heartburn	Miss Minnie Wood

CORNET SOLO,   Prof. Charles Bierwith

MISS BELLE LAVERDE,
Will sing the Temple of Fame, 2d Degree East Moon and That's Where Your'e Wrong

KING SARBRO
The Japanese Potentate, in his Perilous Slide for Life.

OVERTURE, - - - - - Orchestra

The whole to conclude with Laughable Sketch, entitled
ARE YOU GOING TO THE BALL THIS EVENING?
YES, THIS EVENING!

Door Keeper	NED WEST
Manager	Harry Wood
Dog	Punch Marsh

Other Characters by the Company.

Entire change of Programme Thursday Evening January 13th.

Grand Complimentary Benefit Tendered to HARRY and MINNIE WOOD, Thurs'y Afternoon and Even'g Jan. 13. A host of Volunteers

ACT TWO

The Great Levantine

Staid Albany, New York, with horse-cars and cabs, was the place where Fred F. Proctor, known professionally as F. F. Levantine, settled on his return from Europe. He immediately looked about for a theatrical engagement, and within a few days he accepted a small-circuit tour in and around Albany though it seemed like starting all over again and on a scale that was petty compared to the bookings he had just had in Europe. But, though European trips gave him a wealth of ideas, he had little actual cash left after traveling and living costs. His plan was to lay up some capital to open his own theatre. He was willing to do anything to raise capital. For a time he was without funds. The backwoods theatres didn't always pay their way, and sometimes he had to crawl into a hayloft to sleep and go without his supper.

One of these nights he never forgot. He had been playing in Catskill, N. Y., and was scheduled back in Albany for a trip north the next day. After the performance, he took his place at the end of the pay-off line of performers, musicians and ushers, laughing and joking about the small Catskill audience. When it was his turn to get paid, the manager lifted his hands in despair.

"It's terrible, Mr. Levantine. The take tonight wasn't enough to pay the salaries. The money is all gone. I can let you have it next week if you'll come back a week from tonight, or let me know where I can send it to you." The manager turned his pockets inside out, and wound up with: "The thing that hurts is that you, the great equilibrist, the hit of the show, the feature that drew everybody—it's YOU that doesn't get paid!"

Proctor shrugged his shoulders, patted the manager on the shoulder, trying to ease his embarrassment, and walked down to the West Shore railroad tracks. His strong body didn't go back on him, and by tramping the ties he made Albany on the next day.

One time he had to give up the furnished room and sleep in the theatre, but that did not bother him—he actually said it was a convenience to be so near the place where he worked.

Mr. Proctor was fond of telling about the time when his landlady took pity on him. She knocked on his door and offered him a can of pork and beans she had just opened. "My dear young man," she said, "you look awfully weak and undernourished. I imagine you could use some substantial food." Mr. Proctor always added, "But the kind-hearted landlady forgot to give me a spoon to eat them with."

His contract with the small circuit manager was non-exclusive, so he was free to play any additional engagements he could find. A newspaper clipping that describes an Elks Benefit in Boston on January 8, 1880, says that Fred F. Levantine was seen in "feats of equilibrium."

Fred Proctor's first business venture *per se* was launched before he went to the Continent. In 1876 he was a performer in Montgomery Queen's Circus, and he purchased the popcorn, candy and lemonade rights for the circus. So—besides performing as an equilibrist—he pushed in among the crowds, hawked refreshments, and was soon saving up capital for his cherished dream of theatre ownership and promoiton. He often remembered in later years how unsympathetically many performers he had known received his suggestion that a person owed it to himself to save in prosperous times to build for the future. While he was plying his concession with the circus and at the same time playing the small-time circuit, many of his prosperous actor friends were devoting all their spare time to card-playing.

Mr. Proctor, billed as Fred Levantine, appeared with other circuses—D. W. Stone's (in 1878), Adam Forepaugh's, and L. B. Lent's. He was soon being featured on billboards and programs as "World's Wonder, F. F. Levantine, Equilibrist, In His New and Marvelous Entertainment." Posters showed him gaily dressed and standing perched with one foot upon a great sphere. Splendidly colored banners bore flaring headlines: "The Great Levantine, at the Capitol Theatre." The handbills described his great agility in balancing and juggling globes, pyramids and barrels, and he was billed as the World's Champion Equilibrist.

Prof. George C. D. Odell's *Annals of the New York Stage*, lists the following appearances of Fred F. Levantine (F. F. Proctor) in New York and Brooklyn between September 1875 and January 1882; for the last three and a half years of this time he repeatedly appeared as a member of the team of Levantine and Earle. The following list is only for his solo billings.

Olympic Theatre	Sept. 1875 Globe and barrel equilibrist "was bright star"
" "	Mar. 1876
Theatre Comique	Nov. 1876 On same bill with Nat C. Goodwin
" "	Dec. 1876
Tivoli Theatre	Oct. 1877
Theatre Comique	Feb. 1878
Park Theatre	Feb. 1878 Among "an astonishingly generous supply of 'headliners'"
Theatre Brighton	Sept. 1878
Aberle's Tivoli	Sept. 1878
Theatre Comique	Oct. 1878
Novelty Theatre	Nov. 1878 Billed as "World's Champion Equilibrist"

Aberle's New Theatre   Dec. 1878
Niblo's Garden   Mar. 1879   Billed as a specialty
                                            performer
Olympic Theatre (Brooklyn)   Mar. 1879
Aberle's Tivoli   Apr. 1879
Tony Pastor's Theatre   Apr. 1879   On same bill with
                                            Pat Rooney and his Star Troupe
Lent's N.Y. Circus   Oct. 1879
London Theatre (Bowery)   Nov. 1879
Booth's Theatre   Feb. 1880
Academy of Music (Brooklyn)   Apr. 1880
Aberle's New Theatre   Sept. 1880
Harry Miner's Theatre (Bowery) Oct. 1880 and Feb. 1881

The Levantine and Earle references:

Harry Miner's New Theatre
  (Bowery)   July 1878
Olympic Theatre (Brooklyn)   Aug. 1878
Novelty Theatre (Williamsburg) Sept. 1878
Stadt (Windsor) Theatre   Dec. 1878
London Theatre (Bowery)   Apr. 1879
Aberle's New Theatre   Sept. 1879
Harry Miner's Theatre (Bowery) Oct. 1879
Hyde & Behman's Theatre   Dec. 1879
American Theatre   Dec. 1879
Harry Miner's Theatre (Bowery) Mar. 1880
"   "   "   " Oct. 1880
Wagner's Laurel Hill Assembly
  Rooms (Long Island City)   Oct. 1881
National Theatre (Bowery)   Dec. 1881
Hyde & Behman's Theatre   Jan. 1882

* * *

The time had finally come, in 1880, the year of the Boston Elks Benefit, when Mr. Proctor, now nearly thirty, had the capital for his start in show business. With a thousand dollars in a savings bank, he set out to shop for a theatre in Albany the same way he had shopped for a gymnasium in Boston years before. He walked through the maze of downtown streets, and when he came to Green Street he felt his search was over. He walked into the Green Street Theatre. He was familiar enough with the place, for he had appeared on the stage, he knew its peculiar acoustics and its skimpy dressing rooms.

The owner of the Green Street Theatre naturally thought that the ruddy-faced young man with the stocky build and friendly manner had come in to arrange a booking. He was surprised when Fred said, "I've come to buy the place."

The deal was made simply, without haggling or bickering of lawyers.*

Mr. Proctor renamed the house Levantine's Theatre; and it was later called the Gayety. Mr. Proctor pitched in himself, swept the lobby and sidewalk, helped push scenery around, made up some handbills, and went out into the street to distribute them. He called in a plumber named Wallen, who did wonders in rehabilitating the old showhouse. Mr. Proctor took an immediate liking to him. One day, when the plumbing was nearly done, he asked the plumber, "Mr. Wallen, do you know of a good, intelligent boy who'd be interested in a job as usher for this theatre?"

"Yes, I do," said Mr. Wallen. "I have several of them in my own family."

"Well, then, bring one of them down with you in the morning," Mr. Proctor told him.

That was the beginning of the Wallens' life-long association with Mr. Proctor. The plumber brought his son, George, then twenty, to the theatre next morning. Mr. Proctor, after one look at him, said he'd be delighted to have him work with him

* The *Dictionary of American Biography* in its article on F. F. Proctor errs in saying that he did not buy the theatre outright. And that article gives the date incorrectly as 1886.

and would make him treasurer because he was older and more intelligent than was necessary for the ushering job.

Two years later, when Mr. Proctor acquired the Pearl Street Theatre in Albany, he told Mr. Wallen he could use two more boys if they were anything like George. Thereupon Mr. Wallen brought in his sons Harry and Clarence, and they were installed as usher and treasurer, respectively, of the Pearl Street Theatre. The three Wallen brothers remained with Mr. Proctor as long as he lived. When Mr. Proctor died in 1929, George had rounded out forty-nine years of continuous service, and Harry and Clarence each forty-seven years. George Wallen was advanced in the Proctor organization through several promotions, finally becoming secretary and treasurer of the various F. F. Proctor corporations. In 1907, Harry was made treasurer of the United Booking Offices of America, of which Mr. Proctor was vice-president. Clarence Wallen became vice-president of the F. F. Proctor corporation and succeeded to the presidency upon Mr. Proctor's death. Both he and his brother George, by Mr. Proctor's will, became trustees of the Proctor estate. George died in October 1941, at the age of eighty.

One of the best-remembered stories of his early hardships as a theatre manager tells of Mr. Proctor's four-fold job in his first playhouse: he was general house manager, bookkeeper, bill-poster and circularizer. And, in addition, he acted on the stage of his own theatre as an acrobat, just as Tony Pastor always had a prominent spot on his own bills.

During the noon hour, Mr. Proctor walked along State Street and distributed handbills. After this noon-hour circularizing, he would rush to the theatre, slip into his tights and give his matinee performance as "The Great Levantine, Sensational Equilibrist." He helped his other performers with their acts and then went to his business office where he counted up his matinee take and completed the books. Then he gathered up another bundle of handbills and went on his six o'clock route to catch people in the homeward rush hour. He stationed himself at a busy spot where multitudes alighted from the horse-drawn street cars, and each passenger received a handbill of Levantine's Novelty Theatre almost as certainly as if it were a street-car transfer ticket.

A feature of his first theatre that Mr. Proctor hadn't bargained for was the bar. Before he closed the deal for the theatre, he discussed the possibility of taking out the bar, but he learned that, besides losing the profits from the drinks sold there, he would also lose at the box-office, for the attendance, largely male, would fall off considerably without a bar. He kept the bar, and in 1881 his handbills proclaimed:

> At our temple of fun, we do all to please;
> You can smoke your cigar and drink at your ease.

In this first theatre he started sloganeering, calling it "Preeminently the Greatest Resort in Albany for Pleasurable Enjoyment."

It was at this time that Mr. Proctor, through a chance meeting with M. B. Leavitt, who had "discovered" him and who was an influential manager, got valuable fundamental information about entertainment management—if we are to take at face value Leavitt's story told in his book,* under the caption "I Inadvertently Give Fred Proctor A 'Tip.'"

One day when Proctor was on the platform at Albany waiting for the train to New York, a ponderous man grabbed him by the shoulder and exclaimed, "Well, I'll be, if it isn't Fred Levantine Proctor—my own discovery!"

"Hello there! How have you been?" replied Proctor, in his soft, distinct voice.

Leavitt led him a few steps toward the station restaurant and urged: "Come on inside, old man. Have breakfast with me. I

---

* *Fifty Years in Theatrical Management.*

see that you are getting the train to New York. We can make it together."

As they sat down, Fred Proctor began:

"Say, Mr. Leavitt, I'm so glad that I met you just now. I've always marveled at your vast theatrical empire. How is it possible for you to operate so many theatres and shows at a time? Why, I'm at wit's end running my little Novelty Theatre."

Mr. Leavitt leaned across the table and explained simply and briefly his system, his forms of organization, his policies, his outstanding failures and his marked successes. He gave Proctor, in the restaurant and on the trip down to New York, a remarkable summary and outline of his experience and knowledge.

Years later, Leavitt met Proctor again when he was operating his own system of theatres, and said, "Well, Fred, I see you are very successful." Proctor replied, "Yes. I never forgot the conversation we had at the depot restaurant at Albany. It was ever in my mind, and I was determined to follow your example, using your great experience as my model." The compliment was highly gratifying to Leavitt. Maybe both Leavitt and Proctor exaggerated the importance of the conversation, but certainly it shows that Mr. Proctor was quick to learn from others.

In 1884, with W. C. Coup, brother-in-law of P. T. Barnum, Mr. Proctor leased the Theatorium and grounds near the Genesee Falls in Rochester, N. Y., and made one of the finest and most elaborate show grounds in the country. Five large halls were filled with a collection of curiosities and rare specimens, and in the main auditorium, a stock comic opera company with some of the best-known stars of the day presented operettas. The venture was a tremendous success, and for several weeks the attendance was limited only by the capacity of the auditorium.

About this time Henry R. Jacobs came to Albany. He had

owned a small dime museum in Park Row, New York City, and then he began putting on tent shows in smaller cities and giving a big show for a small admission. He made so much money that he was able to lease large theatres and present melodramas and popular comedies at a new low scale of prices, the famous "ten, twenty, thirty" cent shows.

Jacobs' success in Albany was soon felt by Proctor in his theatre on Green Street, and Proctor made overtures to his rival. The resulting firm of Jacobs and Proctor (1884) in the next seven years practically revolutionized the show business in America.

They opened Jacobs and Proctor's Museum on South Pearl and Beaver Streets, where later the DeGraff Building was erected. The ground floor was stores; the second was a museum exhibiting freaks; and the third floor was the theatre where Jacobs and Proctor presented popular-priced drama. On the ground floor, William E. Drislane, Sr., later well known as a merchant on North Pearl Street, ran a general grocery. Mr. Drislane once said, "Mr. Proctor was a good business man; shrewd, alert and a hustler. He was always courteous and anxious to please his public. He laid the foundation of his subsequent large fortune in that museum and theatre upstairs."

With the lease of the Martin Opera House in Albany in 1884, the Jacobs and Proctor chain—the greatest cheap-priced theatrical circuit this country has ever known—was on its way. Managers were enabled to book with them for an entire season over their chain of theatres. Proctor and Jacobs started a theatre in nearly every important city in the land, and in New York, Philadelphia and Chicago, they controlled three or four houses. In all these houses the ten, twenty, thirty cent scale of prices prevailed, and woe to the playhouse and management that attempted to compete with them! Besides the theatres under their control, Jacobs and Proctor organized more than a score of theatrical companies so that profits which otherwise would go to the traveling manager came to the firm.

Under the direction of Jacobs and Proctor, for almost seven years, were presented some of the best variety shows that had been seen in America during that period. Mr. Proctor, at the same time, had his own theatres—as may be seen in the following clipping from a Brooklyn newspaper in 1888.

> The two men who have cut the widest swath in American theatricals during the past few years have separate interests in Brooklyn. In some cities they are partners, in others rivals. It was as Jacobs & Proctor that they came into prominence, and after extending operations in partnership they began to branch out individually. Frederick F. Proctor was the first to settle in this city. His success with the Novelty prompted him to also secure the Criterion, and he now controls both houses, in connection with fourteen others in various cities. Mr. Proctor's advancement has been decidedly rapid. It is not many years ago that he was a performer, while now he directs more enterprises than any other man in the business except his partner. He began modestly as a manager in Albany, which is still the headquarters of his chain of theatres, and where he spends more time than in any other one place, for he is constantly travelling from one city to another. Even with so many irons in the fire this energetic man is constantly on the lookout for new fields of endeavor, and when he makes a bid for a house that he is anxious to get it is pretty hard to compete with him. Next season he will have a New York Theatre. In W. L. Allen and Caleb Woglom Mr. Proctor has two excellent representatives.

* * *

But, like all theatrical crazes, the vogue of the ten, twenty and thirty cent shows eventually declined. Once more Proctor was able to weather adversity, for he had not neglected to lay away money during the fat years of the ten, twenty and thirty.

Shortly afterward, Jacobs and Proctor parted company. In Albany Mr. Jacobs bought from Mrs. Rose Leland the Leland

Opera House, and Mr. Proctor continued at the South Pearl Street stand. In 1889 Proctor purchased the Leland from Mr. Jacobs and at once devoted it to the popular-priced vaudeville that was his special field. Most of the great stars of vaudeville played the old Leland. Maurice Barrymore and Clara Morris, the first legitimate stars to play vaudeville engagements, appeared there in playlets. Here Elsie Janis, as "Little Elsie," imitated famous stars of the day, and Ina Claire as a youngster started in vaudeville. Montgomery and Stone, Lillian Russell, Weber and Fields, Pete Dailey, Sandow and hundreds of other headliners showed there.

A newspaper story of this period illustrates Mr. Proctor's businesslike methods. He had made it a rule at his theatres that no person could pass the doorman without a ticket or pass. One day when he came to Albany and visited the Leland Theatre, there was a new doorman on duty who had never seen Mr. Proctor and did not know the proprietor was in Albany. When Mr. Proctor started to pass the doorman, he said,

"You can't go in without a ticket," and barred his way.

"But I am Mr. Proctor. I own this theatre," was the reply.

"I don't know you," the doorman answered. "My orders are to admit no one without a ticket."

Mr. Proctor had to go to the box office and get the treasurer to tell the doorman who he was. When the doorman began to apologize, Mr. Proctor said gently, "No, you were right. Now I know that I have a good man at the door at the Leland."

* * *

In these early Jacobs and Proctor days in Albany, there was a strange competition one time between Proctor's Leland and Pearl Street Theatres. For the same week, by a peculiar and accidental duplication, the Primrose and West Minstrels were booked for the Leland Theatre and the Thatcher Minstrels for the Pearl Street Theatre. When the situation was discovered and explained to both minstrel outfits, neither company would give in—each group insisted it would play the town whether or not the other was there. It was an opportunity to demonstrate which had the bigger entertainment appeal.

The newspapers made repeated and extensive comment on the situation, particularly after it assumed the proportions of a feud. Both groups staged their own street parades with banners, elaborate uniforms and impressive bands. One of the companies hired outside musicians to make a more impressive showing, but the ruse was tipped off to the rival company, which then also added to its musical contingent.

With all the newspaper ballyhoo, the interest of the public was aroused to high pitch. The Leland, featuring the more famous Primrose and West troupe, was sold out before the show opened. The sale of tickets for the Thatcher show at the Pearl Street Theatre lagged.

But, before the night was over, both houses were crowded. When the box offices reported, the take of the Thatcher Minstrels was $300 more than that of the Primrose and West performance, because the Pearl Street Theatre had three hundred more seats than the Leland—1600 to 1300. Admission in both houses ranged from 25 cents to $2.

* * *

Mr. Proctor never built a theatre in Albany, but bought several there. His only Albany holding that he built himself was the Stuyvesant Apartments in Washington Avenue, on the former site of a frame house in which he lived and in which his son, Frederick F. Proctor, Jr., was born.

Ambition continued to be his long suit. No man stood higher in the esteem of Albanians and the theatre world generally than he. Now his thoughts turned to New York City, and he decided to expand in the Metropolitan area.

(END OF ACT 2)

ACT THREE

King of Vaudeville

Now Mr. Proctor moved to the top of the vaudeville profession. Although he frequently told the press "Vaudeville is King," and thus glorified his art and profession rather than himself, few of his contemporaries in 1906 would deny that he was King of Vaudeville—and that meant King of the Theatre.

Those lush days of vaudeville are never to be forgotten with their depths and heights that could accommodate the most fervent imagination. Anyone could thrill to the shows at the Proctor theatres. Sitting in a Proctor audience, anyone could watch the soft stage lights change, hear the most enchanting music, and see stars who had hitherto been available only to the boxholders in the Diamond Horseshoe or to those patient, persevering souls who were willing to stand against a back wall or sit uncomfortably in the top gallery of grand opera houses.

Mr. Proctor had watched his expense account in Albany, he had continued to exercise frugality through the prosperous ten, twenty, thirty days, and now he was ready to build his own first metropolitan theatre—according to his own dreams of the perfect playhouse, regardless of cost. Now the frugality of those early days was to bear new fruit.

In 1886, he took over a theatre at the southwest corner of Broadway and Bedford Avenue in the Williamsburg section of Brooklyn. Under the name of Proctor's Novelty Theatre, it thrived handsomely. In 1887, he added another in Brooklyn—Proctor's Criterion Theatre—and in 1889 took on a third, in the Eastern District of that City.

F. F. PROCTOR

In February 1888, Proctor's Novelty Theatre in Brooklyn charged 10 and 20 cents for admission and it advertised that "any purchaser of a 50 cents or 75 cents ticket will be presented with an order for a town lot 25 x 100 feet."

This clipping from a June 1888 issue of the *Brooklyn Times* describes the substantial success Mr. Proctor had attained after two years in Brooklyn.

There are few managers better known in the United States than Mr. F. F. Proctor, a picture of whom appears at the head of the TIMES' dramatic column to-day. Mr. Proctor is without doubt one of the most progressive men in a profession which commands genius and talents of a high order, and he has reached his present enviable position by his splendid executive abilities, wide powers of discernment and thorough appreciation of what the public demands.

Although not yet in the prime of life, he has inaugurated reforms, provided innocent amusement to hundreds of thousands of persons in their hour of recreation and placed the prices of admission to good attractions on a popular basis. That this is no empty praise may be inferred from the fact that the gentleman is not only manager of the handsome theatre in the Eastern District in this city which bears his name, but also of the model and elegant structure known as the Criterion Theatre, which was built as a double of the Madison Square Theatre, New York. Indeed, it may be said that Mr. Proctor's ventures, all of which have proved successful ones in the best sense of the word, cover a large part of four States, and the list, like that of the securities sold on the New York Stock Exchange, is daily growing larger. . . .

The theatres now under Mr. Proctor's management, together with their seating capacity, are as follows: F. F. Proctor's Brooklyn, E. D., 1,800; Proctor's Criterion, Brooklyn, W. D., 1,000; Grand Opera House, Boston, 3,000; Opera House, Hartford, 1,800; Museum, Albany, 1,600; Opera House, Utica, 1,800; Academy of Music, Rochester, 1,600; Grand Opera House, Syracuse, 1,600; Academy of Music, Wilmington, Del., 1,600; Grand Opera House, Wilmington, Del., 2,200; Opera House, Lancaster, Pa., 1,300; Griswold Opera House, Troy, 1,400; and Twenty-Third Street Theatre, New York,

2,800. In addition to these enterprises Mr. Proctor is the manager of Mr. Charles T. Ellis, who has been starring with remarkable success in "Casper the Yodler."

Mr. Proctor makes his headquarters at Albany and all of his many enterprises make daily returns to the Albany house, while all of the bookings for them are made by Mr. Proctor in person. All the books and accounts are in Manager Wallen's charge. Mr. Wallen, a veteran theatrical man, started with Mr. Proctor in 1879,* and allied himself with the firm of Jacobs & Proctor in 1884.

As manager of his circuit Mr. Proctor is indefatigable. Early every Monday morning he makes a complete tour of the circuit, commencing with Boston, and returning to Albany on Sunday. In Manager Wallen's office a system of accounts prevails that is admirable for its simplicity and completeness. What is known as the date list enables one to see at a glance the bookings of every house on the circuit for the entire season. The list contains thirteen columns, each representing a house whose name appears at the top. Running down the margin appear the weeks in the theatrical season and in the spaces opposite are written the names of the companies. The weekly statements and daily accounts of all the houses are kept in a large double cabinet in which are two series of compartments. In the upper series are filed the daily bills, each house having a separate compartment. These bills are grouped each week, each week's bills being inclosed in a separate envelope. In the lower series are filed the weekly statements, in compartments similarly arranged and marked. By this system the business of any house for any time can be seen at a moment's notice. . . .

* * *

In 1889, Mr. Proctor purchased a site at 141 West 23rd Street (between Sixth and Seventh Avenues) and built a modern theatre there with the finest appointments and perfect acoustics.

"This," he said to his friends, "is an experiment in high-grade legitimate productions." The new house in the heart of

---

* 1880 is the correct date. The newspaper made a mistake.

romantic Chelsea opened with Neil Burgess's first performance of his famous play, "The County Fair," a great success.

At the 23rd Street Theatre Mr. Proctor gave Charles Frohman the first home for his stock company. After "The County Fair," many other early Frohman successes, including his first great financial success, "Shenandoah," were produced there. Klaw and Erlanger's first New York production, "The Great Metropolis," by Ben Teal and George Jessup, appeared there. Other great successes at this playhouse were "The English Rose," "Mr. Wilkinson's Widows," "All the Comforts of Home," "The Lost Paradise" and "Thermidor."

Mr. Gus Edwards' first big act, "Schooldays," with the famous song of the same name, opened at Proctor's 23rd Street Theatre. A Paramount movie, released in 1939, was based on the career of Gus Edwards, and the picture makes it plain that Edwards' song got no attention from the music publishers until his newsboy act clicked at Proctor's 23rd Street.

The character of Proctor entertainment—a family show—is well summarized in the anecdote of the visit paid Mr. Proctor by a well-known New York City judge. On meeting Mr. Proctor, the judge said, "You're just the kind of man I imagined you would be."

Proctor smiled and said, "I hope I am acceptable to you."

"You don't know how acceptable you are," replied the judge. "I've been going to your show every week now for the past two months with my wife and little girl and little niece, because you've got the kind of show that keeps a family together."

Proctor thanked the judge, but the judge interrupted him:

"I want to be thanking you. You've added to my stock in trade as a judge. I'm recommending your theatre for all of my future domestic troubles cases. Men don't go sneaking off alone to corrupt places of entertainment now that you have provided in your 23rd Street Theatre a source of real inspiration and joy."

F. F. Proctor at 18

F. F. PROCTOR AT 21 (IN 1872)

F. F. Proctor in 1905

F. F. Proctor at Miami in 1924

Mr. and Mrs. Proctor, about 1900, on their Central Valley Estate

Mr. Proctor's last Photograph taken when he Retired from Active Control of his Theatres

George E. and
Clarence H. Wallen

Mr. Proctor was quick to notice changes in public taste. His 23rd Street Theatre was in the main shopping district of that time. His past experience had told him that the two-a-day was a greater accommodation for the shopper than the legitimate attractions that played only at night, and he decided that all-star vaudeville was closer to the hearts of the masses than legitimate shows and more adaptable to the two-a-day policy. Then he and Mr. Frohman separated. Mr. Proctor stayed on at the 23rd Street Theatre and Mr. Frohman moved his stock company into the Empire Theatre, built for him by Al Hayman and Frank W. Sanger.

Confining himself now to vaudeville, Mr. Proctor began to realize that it would have to be *all-star* and *continuous*. The first week after the change, there was a slump in business. Proctor was quick to diagnose the trouble.

He told his theatre manager, "Now that we have abandoned the straight legitimate and are resolved to go the vaudeville way—as I am sure we must go if we are to give the masses what they want—we must bring into vaudeville better and more varied talent."

So he began looking about for the better and more varied talent. He had been the first to pay fabulous salaries to induce stars from the legitimate to enter vaudeville. Now he astonished everybody by announcing that he had engaged the famous grand opera tenor Signor Italo Campanini * to sing at his continuous performances. The price was not increased, and even when he offered an operatic company of forty persons and about a dozen good "turns," he continued the old scale of prices.

Mr. Proctor's next step was the opening of the "Ladies Club Theatre," at the 23rd Street, with a daily list of twenty acts from 11 A.M. to 11 P.M. Cards reading "After Breakfast Go to Proctor's and Hear Campanini" were distributed throughout

* He was an older brother of the great conductor, Cleofonte Campanini, and he toured the United States first with Nilsson and then with Patti.

the city. Every shop window, trolley car, hotel news-stand, every elevated train displayed these cards, and this started the vogue of the *continuous* in Greater New York.

One of his greatest advertising slogans at this time—

> After Breakfast Go to Proctor's
> After Proctor's Go to Bed

—impressed upon the public the meaning of *continuous*.

Mr. Proctor's press agent trained two hundred or more parrots to repeat the words, "After Breakfast Go to Proctor's." These birds were offered as prizes to all holders of green admission tickets, and the box office arranged to mix in a certain number of green tickets at each performance.

These methods to impress upon the public that Proctor's was continuous certainly registered. The manager at the 23rd Street never forgot how much it impressed many mothers. Some women sent their children to Proctor's right after breakfast with their lunch in a bundle and told them to stay all day and come home in the evening. And a few even packed up supper for the children and reminded them that they could get drinking water in the theatre. Mothers would sometimes come to the manager and say, "Will you please help me find my children in your theatre? I know they're here, for I sent them here after breakfast and told them to stay all day. It's safer for them in the theatre than in the street." The manager then announced from the stage that Mrs. So-and-So was looking for her family.

"We had a mighty good sprinkling of these children who stayed and stayed," the manager recalled. "But even though these kids saw three shows a day, it didn't work any hardship on us. These young 'guests' filled up only a certain small percentage of seats that the regular audience wouldn't have occupied. So we were glad to have them."

Proctor's Pleasure Palace, on Fifty-eighth Street between Lexington and Third Avenues, built in 1895, was his most important and daring undertaking up to that time. It was a landmark of the middle East Side for many years. The only earlier theatre in the 19th Ward was the Terrace Garden at Fifty-eighth Street and Lexington Avenue. It was Mr. Proctor's idea to build a great amusement palace directly opposite the Terrace Garden. The new house opened with great éclat. Not even in Europe was there a grander combination of inviting amusement halls. The theatre proper was only one of the auditoriums. Even the basement had a finely constructed theatre and stage, and on the roof was an elaborate garden theatre. Adjoining the main theatre on the ground floor was a palm garden large and elaborate enough for a grand opera company.

Here is part of an advance story of the Pleasure Palace from the August 9, 1895, issue of the New York *Morning Advertiser*.

Mr. F. F. Proctor's new colossal and comprehensive playhouse now being erected in Fifty-eighth Street, between Third and Lexington Avenues, and his many theatrical enterprises now running so successfully, naturally suggest queries as to who Mr. Proctor is and was and where he made the wherewithal to own and direct his theatres. . . .

To him alone does the American public owe the establishment of the popular-priced houses, which are now to be found in every large city in the country. The establishing of Proctor's Theatre on West Twenty-third Street, New York, was his most ambitious undertaking and one of the most successful. Many high class dramatic productions were made at this house. In 1892 Mr. Proctor changed the policy of this theatre and gave New York its first continuous offering of light opera and refined vaudeville, especially designed for ladies and children.

Mr. Proctor is a man of pleasing address, very quiet, unostentatious and unassuming. He has a genius for hard work and the mastery of detail. His ventures receive the closest personal attention and his finger is at the public pulse, quick to detect its slightest variation. Mr. Proctor has a palatial home at Larchmont Manor on Long Island Sound, where he has an interesting art collection and many curios collected in every part of the world. There is everything about his charming home life to tempt one to relaxation, but Mr. Proctor is untiring in his devotion to business affairs. Since October last he has been touring the principal cities of Europe in search of new ideas and bent upon obtaining foreign novelties for the amusement of the public.

* * *

This Theatre of Theatres, as it might have been called, was opened on Labor Day of 1894, with a splendid program, the result of Mr. Proctor's European hunt for talent. Broadway prices were charged and Mr. Proctor spared no luxury for his patrons.

The opening night was long to be remembered. The house was competely sold out—at special prices, and among the attractions were George Lockhardt's troupe of comedy elephants, Weber and Fields, Sam Bernard, Lottie Gilson, Rice & Cohen, Lew Dockstader, the operatic baritone William T. Carleton, and many others.

The main theatre of the Pleasure Palace with a program of fifteen acts and a "sacred concert" on Sundays, which appealed to women and children quite as much as to men, was financially sound. But the enterprise as a whole was so elaborate and lavish —with theatre, palm garden, night club and roof garden, all in one—that the overhead was too much for the neighborhood to carry. It was months before the great enterprise began to show a loss, but eventually the inevitable slump came, and the house had an irregular career, going from one style of entertainment to another. The indefatigable showman was compelled to close all but the main auditorium, which he continued for a while. Mr. Proctor was probably twenty years ahead of time in his exploitation of this enterprise.

But Mr. Proctor was not discouraged. In 1898 he opened his first theatre in New Jersey. He had liked Newark in the early days when he was a performer and not a manager. He remarked a greater leisureliness in Jersey and a slower pace of life than in Brooklyn and Manhattan. This, he thought, should mean a greater show attendance. The theatre he built in Newark in 1898, facing the Military Park point where Broad Street and Park Place meet, was so profitable that he could never be induced to sell it.

Lawrence J. Golde, who booked Proctor's 23rd Street and Fifth Avenue Theatres in New York and his Newark theatres, not long ago commented on Mr. Proctor's wide taste in entertainment:

> I remember an interesting departure which Mr. Proctor inaugurated at his 23rd Street Theatre—a sort of triple-threat program of entertainment—when that theatre was suffering a bit by its proximity to his Fifth Avenue Theatre at the corner of Broadway and 28th Street. He said: "Let's put in something entirely new: a stock company running a condensed play for one hour, a vaudeville show running about an hour, and a circus show for an hour." The theatre could hardly accommodate the crowds who came to enjoy this three-hour entertainment. That was typical of his versatility. He was always flexible—never stereotyped.

He once said to me: "I don't see why we can't put in a sort of sketch to open the show, instead of the stereotyped juggling or acrobatic act which has been the vogue for show openings." It has been said that he was partial to good acrobatic acts. He was partial to anything that was really good. He appreciated skill when he saw it. His own vast and colorful background in the acrobatic arts enabled him to know the good ones from the hams. He felt that a good acrobatic act should be shown to advantage—in the middle of the show. That's why even to this day we see them in the middle of shows, whereas in the olden days an acrobatic act was stamped as an opening act.

* * *

In the early nineteen hundreds, Mr. Proctor had served his apprenticeship and journeymanship, so to speak, and he was becoming the veritable master. Vaudeville's heyday was principally due to his theatrical genius. Variety was now becoming a higher art, and snap and polish were replacing crudities and awkwardness. Lillian Russell, Lily Langtry, Henry Miller, Robert Hilliard, Dion Boucicault, Robert Mantell, Charles Hawtrey, William Collier, James T. Power, and many other stars of the legitimate were brought into vaudeville by Mr. Proctor. Headliners—all of them—played his entire circuit. His audiences thrilled to such top-flight artists as The Four Cohans, Jack Norworth and Nora Bayes, Weber and Fields, Marie Dressler, May Robson, Eva Tanguay, McIntyre and Heath, Primrose and West, Joe Welch, Lew Dockstader, Billy Emerson, Sam Bernard, George Thatcher, Gus Hill's Minstrels, Gallagher and Shean, the Floradora Sextette, Pat Rooney, Italo Campanini, Eddie Foy and Family, Vesta Victoria, Vesta Tilley, Annette Kellermann, The Hengler Sisters, Rogers Brothers, Rath Brothers, Gus Williams, Eugene Sandow, Lottie Gilson, Jimmy Thornton, Julian Eltinge, Willie Edouin, Gilmore's Band, James J. Corbett, Fred Walton, Joe Jackson, Billy B. Van, Fay Templeton, Marshall P. Wilder, Sarah Bernhardt, Ada Rehan, Billee Barlow, Edna Wallace Hopper, De Wolfe Hopper, Five Cherry Sisters, Harry Houdini, Yvette Guilbert, Alice and Marie Lloyd, Lafayette the Magician, Modjeska, Mlle. Dazie, Cliff Gordon, Carmencita, Valeska Suratt, James F. Hoey, Gertrude Hoffman, George Hamid, John C. Rice, Charles Grapewin, Ross and Fenton, Carrie De Mar, Jessie Bartlett Davis, and hundreds of others from the regular vaudeville fields.

There were still others who came to the Proctor circuit after being big successes at the famous old Casino Theatre and at Tony Pastor's: Harrington and Hart, Hallen and Hart, Maggie Cline, Louis Mann, Henry Dixey, Della Fox, Thomas Seabrooke, Lillian Russell, William T. Carleton, Delehanty and Hengler, Nat C. Goodwin, Dan Daly, and who knows how many more.

An additional list of Proctor's recruits from the legitimate includes Neil Burgess, Clara Morris, May and Flo Irwin, Rose Coghlan, Gertrude Coghlan, Herbert Kelsey, Amelia Bingham, Mrs. Leslie Carter, Minnie Maddern Fiske, Mrs. Patrick Campbell, George Beban, Dustin Farnum, William Faversham, Maude Adams, Minnie Seligman, Frances Starr, Charles Richman, Blanche Ring, Raymond Hitchcock, Wilton Lackaye, Arnold Daly, Kyrle Bellew, Adele Ritchie, Henrietta Crosman, William Courtenay, Edwin Arden, Florence Reed, Malcolm Williams, Anne Irish, Harry Woodruff, Elita Proctor Otis, and many others.

Before Mr. Proctor's career was ended, he was to bring his thousands of patrons even such latter-day stars as Harry Lauder, Will Rogers, Moore and Littlefield, Rudy Valee, Burns and Allen, Irene and Vernon Castle, Moran and Mack, Jimmy Durante, Joe Cook, The Avon Comedy Four, The Empire City Four, W. C. Fields, Ted Lewis and Band, Ben Bernie and Band, B. A. Rolfe, Joe Frisco, Fritzi Scheff, Frank Fogarty, Fred Bradna, Leo Carrillo—this list, too, is almost endless.

It was in 1900 that Mr. Proctor acquired the incongruously named Fifth Avenue Theatre at Broadway and Twenty-eighth Street. The terms and significance of the deal by which Mr. Proctor took over this theatre, which had been a legitimate house for many years and was the first playhouse of that type to be converted to vaudeville, were detailed in the *New York Herald* of March 4, 1900, along with the news that he was going into Philadelphia.

The announcement made exclusively in the *Herald* of yesterday that the Fifth Avenue Theatre had passed into the control of Mr. F. F. Proctor, the manager of two "continuous performance" houses in New York and a theatre in Albany, by the purchase of Mr. Edwin Knowles' lease, was the sensation of the day in dramatic and vaudeville circles.

The *Herald* is now enabled to announce further that the Gilsey estate has supplemented the Knowles lease (which expires in two years) with a lease for ten years additional direct to Mr. Proctor, which gives him absolute control of the theatre till 1912. . . .

Mr. Proctor has made another quiet, strategic move outside of New York, and while out of town managers presumed that he was sleeping on his Albany holdings and would not enter any other city as a vaudeville theatre rival he has secured a strong footing in Philadelphia. . . .

The *Herald* yesterday received information of this Philadelphia move from one of the gentlemen there concerned in the affair, and upon asking Mr. Proctor's endorsement of the statement he unwillingly confirmed it. He said: . . . "The *Herald* learned of my purchase of the Fifth Avenue lease before I was ready to make it known, and published it; and now it has found out my move upon Philadelphia just as it is being completed! Since the *Herald* puts the direct question to me, I must answer, 'Yes; it is true.' It will probably be settled in a few days whether I take the Park, or accept the offer of a new theatre to be built for me. . . ."

The invasion of the heart of the Broadway theatre district by the prominent "continuous performance" manager, is indeed, a surprise. It was believed that he desired to get on Broadway, but it was not seen where he was to get an opening, as all the theatres were held in hands that were unlikely to surrender them, and were devoted to dramatic or operatic productions. . . .

When it became known that Mr. Proctor had taken the Fifth Avenue, the question was at once asked, "Will he close it to the dramatic companies that have regularly played there, or will he continue its present policy?"

The significance of the question was this: It has been looked on as a theatre in which dramatic companies that do not play in the "syndicate" houses can find an entry into New York. Unless Mr. Proctor made it a dramatic house it closed that place to several well known companies and stars.

It may be said at once that Mr. Proctor will fulfil the contracts for time made by Stuart Robson, who follows Modjeska for three weeks, and Joseph Jefferson, who will play his engagement ending Saturday, May 5. That will be the last dramatic performance at the Fifth Avenue, and on the following Monday Mr. Proctor will reopen the house with high class "continuous" vaudeville. The prices, by the way, will astonish Broadway—fifty cents for the best orchestra seat and twenty-five cents for the balcony. . . .

There have been stories—largely "talk"—of the invasion of New York by some Western syndicate of vaudeville managers.

The securing of the Fifth Avenue by Mr. Proctor—all the other houses being in permanent holding—closes the door to any effort of that sort. . . .

To vaudeville stars it is of importance, too, for with his Twenty-third Street Theatre, the Pleasure Palace, the Fifth Avenue, the Albany house and a Philadelphia theatre, Mr. Proctor has become possessed of a chain of houses that will make a long circuit—enabling him to control high class attractions for long periods and keep them out of rival managers' hands. . . .

The price paid for the house by Mr. Proctor he declined to state, but the *Herald* is able to say that the Gilsey heirs decided to close the negotiations on the basis of a rental of very close to $50,000 per annum for twelve years.

* * *

Edward B. Marks, of the Edward B. Marks Music Corporation, recalls an incident at the Fifth Avenue that illustrates Mr. Proctor's fairness and sense of justice.

I remember an incident in connection with the celebrated colored team of Cole and Johnson. They were closely identified with our firm, as we published all their music including "Under the Bamboo Tree," "My Castle On the River Nile," "Maiden With the Dreamy Eyes," and scores of others. In the old days before Bob Cole passed on, he and Rosamond Johnson, as you may remember, did one of the top-line acts in vaudeville. They were one of the first colored acts to get any recognition, during the same period as Ernest Hogan and Williams and Walker.

Most colored acts at that time were not very welcome, as the race prejudice was still strong against the race. In most theatres, however, both Bob Cole and Rosamond Johnson were well received, being well educated and gentlemen. It happened, however, that at Proctor's Fifth Avenue Theatre a new stage manager began to show a deep prejudice during one of Cole and Johnson's periodic engagements. Right from the first performance of the week, he did everything possible behind the scenes to disturb the act, with all sorts of noises and interferences. In other words, he almost broke up the act several times during the week. After remonstrating once or twice, Cole and Johnson decided that there was nothing to be done and that they had better make the best of it. After the last show of the week, however, after every one else of the performers and stage-hands had said good night, Bob Cole walked up to the stage manager and looking him squarely in the eye, said: "I'm a black man with a white heart—you're a white man with a black heart."

The matter came to my attention the following week and as I was very friendly with young Fred Proctor, I told him the story. He questioned the stage hands and after a thorough investigation found that the stage manager had shown similar prejudice to other acts. When he reported it to his father, the man was fired on the spot.

* * *

Jesse L. Lasky gives his personal recollections of Mr. Proctor and the Fifth Avenue Theatre:

As I was the leading vaudeville producer during the years that Mr. Proctor built the Proctor circuit to its eminent position in vaudeville, I naturally came to know him very well. I was also a close friend of Fred Proctor, his son, who booked many of my attractions for the Proctor circuit.

Probably the most elaborate vaudeville act I ever produced, which was inspired by the success of "The Merry Widow," was called "The Love Waltz." It was an operetta featuring Alfred Kappeler and the beautiful Audrey Maple, and was the most pretentious vaudeville attraction produced up to that time.

"The Love Waltz" was booked to open at Proctor's Fifth Avenue Theatre for one week. After the first performance I received word that Mr. Proctor was so impressed with the production that he had decided to hold the attraction over for a month. This he did, advertising "The Love Waltz" so that it became one of the most successful vaudeville operettas of the day. . . .

It is perhaps due to a lucky combination of theatrical brains and energy that this historic playhouse has been enabled to keep its hospitable doors open even until this late date.

Mr. F. F. Proctor, whose long and honored career in the world of the theatre, has, in associating himself with Mr. E. F. Albee and Mr. J. J. Murdock, the President and General Manager of the Keith Circuit, respectively, formed a combination that assured Fifth Avenue patrons of the very best programs of the amusement world, and since 1900, the year when the name F. F. Proctor was first placed over the Fifth Avenue, the house has been accorded a patronage that has made it one of the most eminently successful theatrical enterprises in America. And this, despite the fact that every other neighboring theatre has had its walls razed to make way for the uptown march to new theatre districts. . . .

America's Most Noted Theatre

Although the Fifth Avenue Theatre is in its strictest sense just arrived at the fiftieth milestone in its history, the ground upon which this famous theatre stands was, for several years previous, the home of some of New York's most celebrated and time-honored theatrical institutions. The first theatrical structure reared on this property was known as Apollo Hall, or Ferrero's Dancing Academy, and was erected by Peter Gilsey, opening its doors on October 16, 1868, with a concert by Jerome Hopkins. The hall faced on 28th Street and was two stories in height, with the upper floor being used for concerts and civic events, while the theatre was on the lower floor. The name of the building was next changed to Newcomb's Hall and reopened on April 17, 1871, with Billy Arlington's minstrels. The name of the building was then changed to St. James Hall and started with a variety policy on October 23, 1871. Steele Mackaye first displayed his Delsarte system of acting here. . . .

New Fifth Avenue Theatre

The opening of the New Fifth Avenue Theatre on December 3, 1873, under Augustin Daly's management is regarded as one of the most noteworthy events in New York's theatrical history, and was really the beginning of the present "Fifth Avenue," which on December 3, 1923, celebrates a Golden Jubilee it can well be proud of.

The address delivered at this opening was penned by no less a personage than Oliver Wendell Holmes, and the play—one written especially for the opening—was "Fortune" by Albery. The opening was also made noteworthy by the fact that the first satin drop curtain ever shown in a theatre was used here. . . .

Booth at the Fifth Avenue

On October 25, 1875, Edwin Booth, then the foremost actor of the American stage and one of the world's greatest tragedians, opened an engagement in "Hamlet," to one of the most extraordinary greetings every accorded an actor. Mr. Booth played during the fours weeks following: "Hamlet," "Othello," "Richard II," "The Merchant of Venice," "King Lear," "The Taming of the Shrew," "The Apostate," "The Stranger," "Richelieu" and "The Lady of Lyons." . . .

The gross receipts of Booth's performances were $47,909, or an average of $1,597 for the thirty performances. . . .

In August, 1875, when Augustin Daly had taken the entire Fifth Avenue stock company on a tour to San Francisco, the theatre was occupied by a troupe known as "The Vokes," consisting of Frederick, Fawdon, Jessie, Victoria and Rosina Vokes. Among other plays, they put on "A Bunch of Berries" and "The Belles of the Kitchen" after a short engagement by the balance of Daly's company. . . .

Mr. Daly withdrew from management of the Fifth Avenue on September 15, 1877. . . .

Bronson Howard, the playwright, was discovered by Mr. Daly, and the immediate success of Howard's play "Saratoga" landed him in the first rank of reigning playwrights.

Mr. Daly Leaves

At the termination of Mr. Daly's occupancy, the house was given over to opera, stock star and combinations. On August 23, 1880, the house opened under the name of Haverly's Fifth Avenue Theatre, when a stock star season was inaugurated, Lawrence Barrett being among the stars who appeared here at that time.

The name was next changed to Stetson's Fifth Avenue Theatre on September 11, 1882, when John Stetson took the house and inaugurated a stock season.

On September 23, 1886, Sir Arthur Sullivan of Gilbert and Sullivan led the Fifth Avenue Orchestra at the opening of "The Mikado," and Robert B. Mantell made his debut as a star at this theatre on December 13, 1887.

On May 1, 1888, the house again underwent a change of name when it became Tompkins' Fifth Avenue Theatre.

Miner's Fifth Avenue was the next name employed, when on August 25, 1890, Mr. Miner leased the house which was, at that time, devoted to traveling attractions. . . .

On January 8, 1891, the Gilsey Estate started a large new house which is the present structure. . . . Elenora Duse, Italy's foremost tragedienne, made her first American appearance in "Camille" during this period, at the Fifth Avenue, and Richard Mansfield, then America's foremost actor, opened on October 4, 1897, in "The Devil's Disciple."

. . . F. F. Proctor took possession of the Fifth Avenue Theatre on Sunday, May 6, 1900, completely renovated the house in 24 hours and opened on the following day, May 7. The last engagement in the house previous to Mr. Proctor's opening was Joe Jefferson, whose engagement marked the closing of the former "legitimate" policy.

The house reopened with continuous vaudeville policy, the first Broadway house to offer that style of entertainment. This continued for about two years during which time there appeared only the very best feature acts, such as DeWolfe Hopper, Thos. K. Seabrooke, Dan Daly, Robert Hilliard, Henry Miller and others. The next change was to an all-star stock company with high class vaudeville between the acts, which lasted for over four years.

During that time most of the best known actors and actresses on the legitimate stage appeared in one or another of the plays produced under the stage direction of Hugh Ford. These are a few of the artists, well known then and many of them starring now—Amelia Bingham, Wilton Lackaye, Minnie Seligman, Blanche Bates, Jessie Bonstelle, Florence Reed, Frances Starr, Charles Richman, Charles Abbe, Edwin Arden, Paul McAllister, Malcolm Williams, James Young, Arnold Daly, etc. From 1906 to 1913 this theatre ran a straight two-a-day vaudeville policy and in the fall of 1913 a programme of moving pictures was arranged and presented to the public, this being one of the first three theatres in New York to attempt the presentation of the feature picture that was at that time just coming into popularity. The first bill was Blanche Sweet in "Judith of Bethulia"—since considered by many one of the best pictures ever made. One more year passed and Mr. Proctor then saw the growing demand for vaudeville and this theatre once more became a popular priced vaudeville house playing the best in that line. In spite of the fact that the neighborhood theatres have closed, including Daly's, Wallack's, Weber and Field's Music Hall and The Bijou, and in spite of the fact that the retail shopping district has removed from that section uptown, the public still continues to come to The Fifth Avenue, where Mr. William H. Quaid, House Manager for the past ten years, is ably carrying out Mr. Proctor's policies and keeping the programs up to the typical Keith standard.

* * *

Lawrence Golde recalls an incident that illustrates Mr. Proctor's practical turn of mind and his thought for employees.

During a slack season at his Fifth Avenue Theatre, he once made the suggestion that expenses might be cut a bit at that theatre by reducing the orchestra by three men. He said: "For instance, take out the bass viol." The manager remarked that if those several pieces were cut out of the orchestra there would be a large unuseable vacant space at each end of the orchestra pit. Mr. Proctor told him to just get a few beautiful big palm trees and place them in the vacant spots. And he suggested that the three musicians be switched to another of his theatres where business was booming and the orchestra needed amplification.

Hardly two months had passed after Mr. Proctor acquired the famous Fifth Avenue Theatre when he staked out a new claim for himself by bringing into his fold an important playhouse on 125th Street. This link in his chain was reported, six years later, to have yielded him well over a million dollars in profits. A story about this deal in the *New York Herald* of May 19, 1900, gives a good insight into Mr. Proctor's methods of building his chain, as well as the high regard in which he was held by the principals with which he dealt in some of his biggest transactions:

> East side, west side,
> All around the town.

So ran the old vaudeville refrain of a decade or more ago, and it now applies to the spread of vaudeville itself—especially the Proctor vaudeville. While the merry war of the "continuous" magnates is going on in Boston; while "Jigg and Joggs," the "artistic comedy sketch duo," are wondering whether they will draw two or three hundred dollars next season, or, in the event of a "trust," secure good jobs as motormen; while the Western magnates, headed by Kohl, Shea and Moore, are disputing every inch of ground with Keith, Behman and Albee of the East—while all this is going on, Mr. F. F. Proctor and his wideawake lieutenant, Mr. J. Austin Fynes, seem to have stolen quite a march upon their rivals in the variety business.

Late yesterday afternoon contracts were signed by Mr. Proctor by which he has acquired for a term of more than five years the valuable theatre and business properties in 125th Street, running back to 124th Street, now known as Miner's 125th Street Theatre, and formerly called the Columbus. The lease, which is said to involve an annual rental of about $25,000, also includes the stores on each side of the theatre and the five stories above, now devoted to various uses. Mr. Proctor will take immediate possession.

Mr. McCreery's Reason for Leasing

The lease of the theatre is recorded in the name of William Johnston, but it was ascertained last night by the *Herald* that Mr. Johnston represented Mr. James McCreery, the well known dry goods merchant of this city. Mr. McCreery sailed for Europe early this morning. Late last night he said:

"It is true that I have leased the 125th Street theatre to Mr. Proctor. Since it became known that the property was in the market, I have had numerous offers for it, but upon careful investigation I decided to turn it over to Mr. Proctor, with whose other New York theatres I am quite well acquainted. Mr. Proctor, I am sure, will duplicate his downtown success in Harlem. I have great faith in his energetic and clean methods."

Mr. Fynes, speaking for Mr. Proctor, said: "This move gives us four New York houses all devoted to continuous vaudeville in addition to the Albany house, making five consecutive weeks we can offer performers with practically no railroad expense. The best of these performers we can play twice or three times a year, so that we can practically control any 'star' by booking him or her for fifteen or twenty weeks in New York alone. . . .

"We shall open the 125th Street house in September. We will use the summer for the purpose of an extensive overhauling of the property. It will be conducted on the same policy that has been so successful at the Fifth Avenue, the Twenty-third Street and the Fifty-eighth Street Proctor houses—that is, continuous performance of high class vaudeville at very low prices. We feel sure that Harlem and upper New York will welcome a Proctor house. Of course, there will be no smoking or drinking permitted. The stars who play at the Fifth Avenue will go direct to 125th Street. The bookings for the season are practically completed."

* * *

But acquiring these theatres to strengthen his circuit was, of course, only one phase of Mr. Proctor's vast operations. To keep these theatres supplied with the world's best talent he had

NEW BOWERY THEATRE

SOLE PROPRIETOR.................................Mr. J. W. LINGARD
Stage Manager..................................Mr. N. B. Clarke

CHANGE OF TIME.
DOORS OPEN AT 1-4 BEFORE SEVEN.   CURTAIN RISES AT 1-4 BEFORE EIGHT.

PRIVATE BOXES......$5   ORCHESTRA......50 CTS.   BOXES......25 CENTS
BALCONY CHAIRS...75 CTS.   RESERVED SEATS...50 "   AMPHITHEATRE....15

The Great Drama of

CAPTAIN MACHEATH
THE HERO OF HOUNSLOW HEATH.

Engagement for Six Nights Only, of

HARRY LESLIE,
THE HERO OF NIAGARA!
Grand Ascension
FROM THE STAGE TO THE BACK OF THE GALLERY.

Wednesday Eve'g, Oct. 17, 1866
The Performance will commence with the Famous Drama, in Three Acts, entitled

CAPT. MACHEATH
Or, the Heroes of Hounslow Heath.

Capt. Macheath, the Highwayman............Mr. W. H. Whalley
Peachem, an old Fence...............................Mr. Glassford
Filch, a Clyfaker............Mr. Belvill Ryan	Jemmy the Faker........Mr. W. Wanton
Bag Shot Bill..Mr. Pearson
Ben Budge..........................} Highwaymen {..................Mr. Wright
Mat o'the Mint......................of Capt. Macheath's Gang.........Mr. Hart
Nimming Ned...Mr. Baker
Lord Percy Glynn, Captain of the Black Riders of Hounslow Heath......Mr. Seubert
Lord Archibald, the Monarch of the Night.....................Mr. G. W. Thompson
Lord Fatscults Brooke...Mr. Wheeler
Adrian...........................Mr. Asbury Dowd	King George II...........Mr. N. B. Clarke
Lady Elinor Wayne.............Miss Sarah Steele	Lurline................Miss Fenton
Polly Peachem..................Miss Violet Campbell	Mrs. Peachem........Mrs. Glassford
Lucy Lockit.....................Miss M. Hearie	Barbara..................Mrs. Bowe

SCENERY, INCIDENTS, &c.

ACT I—Flash Ken. Solo and Chorus. Jemmy the Faker and the Gang. The Captain takes the Road. Scene 2—Peachem's House. The Lost of Elinor Wayne. THE ARREST OF THE HIGHWAYMAN. TABLEAU. Scene 3—VAUXHALL GARDENS. The Chief of the Black Riders and the Highwayman. THE WAGER. Abduction
ACT II—Scene 1—Palace of George the Second. Scene 2—THE CONVICT'S CELL. The Highwayman's Sweetheart. FILCH, THE CLIMBER. He breaks into the Prison. RESCUE OF MACHEATH. ANIMATED TABLEAU.
ACT III—Sun Yard of Peachem's. Clyfaker's Holiday. Scene Last—The Hut on Hounslow Heath. Rescue of Elinor by Macheath. THE HUT BLOWN UP. HIGHWAYMAN PARDONED. DEATH OF THE BLACK RIDER. TABLEAU.

LESLIE
Will make his **GRAND ASCENSION ON A SINGLE ROPE**, from the **STAGE TO THE EXTREME HEIGHT OF THE THEATRE**, and returning, at the same time performing his **WONDERFUL FEATS, Fifty Feet High**; astonishing to every beholder, and which have been pronounced to be unequaled by any other artist in the World.

Concludes with the Immense Drama of the

GOLD SEEKERS
OR, MARTELLI OF ANZASKA.

Martelli..............Mr. W. H. Whalley	Nicola....................Mr. Wright
Francisco...}Gold Seekers{...Mr. S. W. Ryan	Pietro................Mr. Belville Ryan
Mayro..........................Mr. Wheeler	Servant.................Mr. Baker
Antonio........................Mr. Dowd	Leila..................Miss Deavill
Bartolo......................Mr. Glassford	Annette..............Miss Campbell
Ricardo......................Mr. Seubert	Guests, Peasants, Minstrels, &c.

An elapse of one year is supposed to take place between the First and Second Acts.

Torrey Brothers, Printers, 13 Spruce St. N. Y.

National Varieties

Cor 49th St. & 8th Ave., opp. 8th Ave. R. R. Depot.

Wm. Rehlsen................Business Manager | Prof. P. W. Turnbull......Leader of Orchestra
Frank A. McClane............Stage Manager | John Blunt............Master of Properties

Balcony Reserved for Ladies
"UNDIMINISHED SUCCESS!"

★ OH!  SEE ★

JULY 15th, 16th & 17th, 1878.

☞ Rich, Rare and Racy! ☜   Come and Judge for Yourselves

The Evening's Entertainment will Eventuate with our

BEAUTIFUL FEMALE MINSTREL SCENE

Bones,	Interlocutor,	Tambo,
Billy Lanning.	F. A. McClane.	Billy Robinson

O o V r E i R g T i U n R a E L..................by Prof. P. W. Turnbull and Orchestra
Under the Snow..Mlle. Romah
Don't Cross the Seas, darling.....................................Miss Lizzie Lanning
Hildebrand Montrose, new version.......................................Billy Lanning
Still I love thee...Little Georgie
The Shady Grove..Billy Robinson
Good bye, Sweet Heart..Miss Lotta Gray
Sweet Chamouni..Miss Minnie Roslanyn
Finale, the Camp Meeting............by Robinson, Lanning and McClane

PART SECOND.--OLIO OF FUN

Overture. "La Traviata," de Verdi.............   Orchestra

The Moon is out to-night, so is
MISS LIZZIE LANNING

| His Specialty | **BILLY ROBINSON** | The Essence |

The Little Pet
LITTLE GEORGIE
In her Aristocratic Song and Dance, Pretty Dittle Blue-eyed Stranger.

| Her Irish | **MLLE. ROMAH** | Character Songs |
| As the | **BILLY LANNING** | Black and Tan |

Overture, "I Puritani," Beleni ...   .   P. W. Turnbull and Orchestra

The Artist's Studio,
By the justly celebrated
NATIONAL ART PICTURE TROUPE,
Arranged and Directed by F. A. McClane. The Light effects by Wm. Rehlsen.

1. The Battle. 2. After the Battle. 3. The Stray Shot. 4. Love, Hate and Jealousy. 5. Jealousy and Crime. 6. The Battle. 7. Dissapointment. 8. The Three Graces. 9. The Last Whoop. 10. The Nations Dependants.

All among the Straw,

LEVANTINE'S NOVELTY THEATRE.

FRED F. LEVANTINE, Lessee and Proprietor.   E. D. GOODING, Manager.   W. J. HOLDING, Leader of Orchestra.

Vol. I.   ALBANY, N. Y., WEEK ENDING MARCH 19TH. 1881.   No. 1.

PROGRAMME

Monday Evening, March 14, 1881,

AND DURING THE WEEK.

Tuesday and Saturday Matinees

AND GRAND HOLIDAY MATINEE,

St. PATRICK'S DAY!

After the Overture by W. J. HOLDING and Orchestra, the following programme will be presented, commencing with

THE RENOWNED GERMAN TEAM,

MILLS AND WARREN;

In their Comedy, entitled

Schneider, How You Vas?

Introducing witticisms and harmonious singing. These gentlemen are the most finished vocalists in the profession.

MISS JOSEPHINE SHANLEY,

The Empress of Song, whose Ballads and Operatic Selections will be recognized.

Engagement and first appearance in Albany of England's Greatest Musical Sensation Artist,

LUIGI DELL 'ORO!

The most talented and miraculous musical genius on the face of the earth. In all foreign cities LUIGI DELL 'ORO's marvellous entertainment has simply astonished, amazed and delighted his audiences. Embrace the opportunity, and see this European sensational novelty.

MODERN SCHOOL OF ACTING

FIRST PROCTOR (LEVANTINE) PROGRAM

The Great Eccentric BOBBY DAILY.

The Premiers of Musical Comedy,

MR. GUS H. SAVILLE

And the Famous Comedian, Wit and Iunster,

MR. JOHN H. BYRNE,

In their original Comedy Creation,

THE COLLEGE OF MUSIC!

Introducing Solos and Duets on the Xylophone, Hirophone and the famous Deplorated Organ. Mr. Saville's Electric E. Flat Cornet Solos, in which he stands pre-eminently above all rivals, and Mr. Byrne's matchless and incomparable revelations of the mocking bird upon a tin whistle.

MISS POLLY DAILY,

The very best of all the Serio-Comic Vocalists, in choice selections.

LEONARD and FLYNN,

The great Irish team and imitators, who are pronounced second to none.

MUSICAL SELECTIONS,

PROF. HOLDING AND ORCHESTRA.

The entire entertainment terminating with the Laughable Farce of the

Baby Elephant.

JOHN	JAS. BREVARDE.
HENRY	CHAS. SAUTELLE.
DR. GAGEM	GEO. WATSON.
ADAM 4 PAW	WM. GILMORE.

Remember Patrick's Day Matinee!

CURTAIN RISES AT 2.30 AND 8.

PRICES, - - - 15, 25, 35 and 50 Cts.
BOXES, - - - - - - $3 and $4.
SINGLE SEATS IN BOXES, - - 75 Cts.

The Wondrous Anniversary Schedule

Representing a Combination of the Leading Attractions from Mr. Proctor's Circuit, as follows:

Monday, April 9th

Proctor's All-Star Players Arrangement with E. H. Sothern, in **"IF I WERE KING"**	Farewell appearance in America of **HENRI de VRIES** In his famous play, "A Case of Arson"

Tuesday, April 10th

Proctor's All-Star Players In Alice Fischer's Great Success, **"MRS. JACK"**	Special Appearance of **MABEL TALIAFERRO** In garret scene from "Little Princess"

Wednesday, April 11th

Proctor's All-Star Company In Amelia Bingham's Starring Success, **"MLLE. MARNI"**	The International Sensation **"LE DOMINO ROUGE"** (The Girl with the Red Domino)

Thursday, April 12th

Proctor's Harlem Company with James J. Corbett, in **"MR. SMOOTH"**	The Famous English Comedienne **VESTA VICTORIA** In her well-known song successes

Friday, April 13th

Proctor's All-Star Players In Bernard Shaw's play, **"CANDIDA"**	First Appearance Here of **YVETTE GUILBERT**

Saturday, April 14th

Proctor's All-Star Players In Shakespeare's **"The Merchant of Venice"**	The Noted English Pantomimist **FRED WALTON** and his "Toy Soldiers"

Sunday, April 15th
An Extraordinary All-Star Jubilee Concert

NEW BOWERY THEATRE

FOX & LINGARD..................SOLE PROPRIETORS

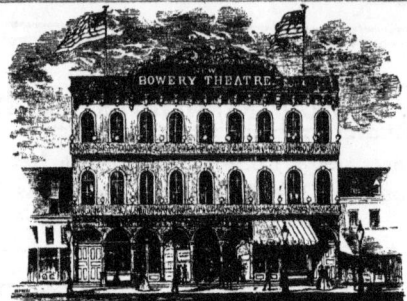

The Grand Comic Pantomime
ENTITLED

HARLEQUIN JACK

THE GIANT KILLER,

Written, composed and produced by

MR. G. L. FOX

Will be performed

EVERY NIGHT THIS WEEK

AND ON SATURDAY AFTERNOON.

THE SCENERY, DRESSES & APPOINTMENTS

Of the most

☞ **GORGEOUS DESCRIPTION !**

SYNOPSIS OF SCENERY AND EVENTS.

Scene 1.—Fairy Abode of Queen Bee and Magical Change to the Village of Normandy......Mr. R. S. Smith

The assembling of the Fairies. Grand Ballet and Chorus, "Queen of the Magical Islands." Arrival of the Fairy Queen in a Golden Bee Hive. The Guild wants a Wife. The terms and MAGICAL CHANGE to

Scene 2.—The Village of Normandy. The Lovers. A stoney hearted father.
The Blacksmith's Apprentice. Mishaps of a Breakfast Table. A Juvenile Travelers. Appearance of Queen Bee in the disguise of a Merchant. Jack receives the three magic gifts: THE INVISIBLE CAP, THE SWORD OF SHARPNESS and the SHOES OF FLEETNESS. Dreadful appearance of the monstrous Giant Gorgibuster, who bears off Sybil.

Scene 3.—The Giant Gorgibuster's Castle...Mr. R. S. Smith
Chorus, old Tune to a new Song, "DIXIES LAND." Fright of the Peasants. Sybil still in the power of the Giant. Heroic conduct of Jack who resolves to conquer the Giant.

Scene 4.—Interior of the Giant's Castle...Mr. R. S. Smith
Ralpho and Hudibras in the Giant's vacuum Sanctorum. The Giant's returns from abroad.

Fe Fi Fo Fum,
I smell the blood of an Englishman,
Let him be alive, or let him be dead,
I'll grind his bones to make my bread.

Horrible fear of Ralpho and Hudibras. Jack gains access to the Castle, disguised as a Pilgrim. A good night's rest. Jack too much for the Giant. Combat between Jack and Gorgibuster. Triumph of Jack and death of the Giant. Appearance of the Guild, determined on the abduction of Sybil. A friend in need. Magical Transformation to

Scene 5.—Queen Bee's Palace of Pleasure...Mr. H. Hilliard

TRANSFORMATION OF THE CHARACTERS:

Clown...Mr. G. L. Fox
Pantaloon..Mr. C. K. Fox
Harlequin..Mr. W. Stanton
Columbine...Miss A. Price

Pot ahead. Merry go round. Catch me if you can. Off we go.

Scene 6.—Panoramic view of New York Harbor..................................Mr. R. S. Smith
Harlequin and Columbine seek shelter in the Hotel. Clown and Pantaloon in pursuit. A new species of irying constitutions. Clown takes them as they come. Peeling a lobster under difficulties. A bit as good as a mile. Great vacuum ball feat. Look out for your back.

Scene 7.—Interior of Hotel, no where's in a Liquor.
Clown and Harlequin in accord. Where shall I dine? A perambulating tablecloth. A travelling fire place. Hot cake for the Pantaloon. Thrilling effects of gunpowder tea. Exchange no robbery. Heads I win, and tails you lose. A Pig's head for a Clown's.

Mazurka...Mr. W. Stanton and Miss A. Price

Scene 8.—Rail Road Depot, Bergen..Mr. R. S. Smith
Be in time. The train's about starting. Pleasant travelling on Cupid's car. Flight of Harlequin and Columbine. Clown and Pantaloon in pursuit on an Express Engine.

Scene 9.—Rustic view. On we go. Cupid's train ahead. Clown behind on the home Stretch.
Pedestrianism runs mad. Reviewing house, (half paint). Stationary in Building. Telescopic house. What's the new? Med ball. Take a horn.

Scene 10.—Rosenzweig's Cigar Store in Chatham Street........................R. S. Smith
Punch at the port. Up to snuff. Magic demijohn. Clown takes an aerial flight on a cork. Big cigars, cheap for the honey. Harlequin disappears through the figure of Punch. "Plan out." Pantaloon tries and ditto ditto. No go. "Short cut." Punch indignant and gives Clown a gentle blot with a foot in the rear. Pig tail. A game at chequers. Getting in jail. Here comes the Police.

Scene 11.—Gisie's Hat store and Zacharie's Perfumery store in the Bowery......R. S. Smith
Row with the Police and general scrimmage.

Scene 12.—Interior of Varick's Hair Dressing Saloon, New Bowery Theatre.......R. S. Smith
A travelling Hat. A clean shave. Expedition, four at once; look out for your nose. No smoking allowed. Harlequin leaps through Varick's plate. Clown and Pantaloon in pursuit through the same aperture.

Scene 13.—Baldwin's Clothing Store, Bowery.....................................R. S. Smith
How to dress in cold weather. A shout man made perfect. Off with your clothes; how dampers've got. Down among the dead men. Sudden Storm. Where's my umbrella. Now you see it and now you don't. A short young lady. Devil features want a dwarf. Magical Transformation to

Scene 14.—The Garden of Roses..R. S. Smith
Pleasant fountains. Clown and Pantaloon get a shower bath, grabs, and change to

Scene 15.—Fort Sumpter by Moonlight. Lovers in despair. Clown and Pantaloon on the right track.

More trouble. Appearance of the Guild determined on the possession of Sybil. The Fairy Queen Bee appears and changes to

Scene 16.—The Bower of Queen Bee and the Abode of the Fairies, Painted by...Mr. H. Hilliard

GRAND FAIRY TABLEAU
THE BIRTH OF THE PEACOCK

IN THE BOWER OF QUEEN BEE.

☞ **SATURDAY AFTERNOON**

For the accommodation of Ladies and Children,

JACK, THE GIANT KILLER

AT HALF-PAST 2 O'CLOCK.

New York Herald Job Office, 97 Nassau Street.

not only to corral all of the top-flight performers in America, but to send scouts to Europe and other parts of the world. He searched the proverbial four corners of the globe for talent to play to his audiences. An alert press was not unaware of his all-out campaign to bring the world's greatest actors and actresses to his stages. A typical newspaper item of that period, telling of the Proctor representative's trip to London, Paris, Berlin and Milan, appeared in the *New York World* of November 19, 1900:

> J. Austin Fynes, general manager of the F. F. Proctor Circuit of theatres, returned yesterday from London on the New York. He has been abroad two months securing attractions and looking over the continuous-performance field in London with a view of opening a London house.
> The principal novelty he obtained was Jean Marcelli's "Living Statuary in Bas-Relief," a revival of the living picture idea in a new dress. Marcelli's troupe consists of twenty-five men and women models. They will open at Proctor's Fifth Avenue house on Dec. 10. Among the other performers engaged were Mlle. Claire Delbosq, Gildy Viaz, of the Casino de Paris; Hill and Hill, the Trentanori Sisters, of the London Alhambra; the Fleury Trio, of the Berlin Winter Garden, and the Florenz Troupe, from Milan.

* * *

No one could have been more deserving of personal publicity and yet less interested in it than Mr. Proctor. "Write about my theatres and my shows; forget about me," was his wish in the matter.

The reporters would smile. How could they possibly divorce the man from his works? His name made good copy!

His next great coups were described as follows in the *New York Herald* of February 7, 1901.

> Mr. F. F .Proctor, the impresario of continuous vaudeville, whose energy seems limitless and whose daring and skilful operations have of

recent years kept theatrical experts very busily guessing, is "up and at it" again. Yesterday was a busy day with Mr. Proctor. In the morning he signed a long lease of a big new theatre; in the afternoon he consummated a long cherished plan by which Mr. David Belasco takes what will probably be a conspicuous place on the American vaudeville stage—and that same stage, by the way, is developing into very important proportions these days—just as the *Herald* has all along predicted it would.

Mr. Proctor's new playhouse is the well known Her Majesty's Theatre, in Montreal, Canada. It will on March 4 quietly take its place in the Proctor circuit, which will then consist of six handsome and fully equipped houses, all devoted to continuous vaudeville of the polite order. In this city four Proctor houses are arranged in nice geographical division from Twenty-third Street to 125th Street; in Albany he has long controlled the famous Leland Opera House, and in his acquirement in Montreal he now adds to his chain the newest and handsomest theatre in Canada.

Her Majesty's Theatre was erected less than two years ago, at a cost of about $200,000, by a company of Montreal capitalists, headed by Mr. William Mann, a retired and wealthy contractor. Originally placed in the Frohman-Klaw-Erlanger-Hayman syndicate, it was quite successful until local dissensions caused its management to break with the New York syndicate. It then became the home of an English stock company, and more recently of an American stock company, in each case with varying success. . . .

Mr. Proctor's general manager, Mr. J. Austin Fynes, had this to say at the Fifth Avenue Theatre last night:

"Mr. Proctor some months ago was approached by the owners of Her Majesty's with a proposition to turn the house over to him. Strangely enough, at the same time another syndicate of Montreal business men offered to erect a brand new structure for him in that city. There thus seemed to be such a strong demand for a Proctor vaudeville house that Mr. Proctor naturally concluded the negotiations with no unnecessary delay. The house is handsomely appointed and quite fully equipped, so that it can be opened on March 4 in splendid shape for the real New York continuous. The performers will jump from our Albany house direct to Montreal or vice versa. The prices, I think, will be low enough to surprise the Montreal public, who have heretofore had very little, if any, really good vaudeville. . . .

"The arrangement effected by Mr. Proctor with Mr. Belasco," continued Mr. Fynes, "is likely to be of considerable importance, for it brings to the vaudeville stage for the first time that splendid one act drama, 'Mme. Butterfly.' Mr. Proctor has booked the entire 'Butterfly' production—scenery, costumes, lighting effects, &c.—for a run of several weeks, beginning at his Fifth Avenue Theatre on Monday, February 18. Mr. Belasco's contract with Mr. Proctor calls for Mr. Belasco's own services, and he will personally supervise the revival of his charming little play. He is very much taken with the idea, too, for he has been quietly studying the Proctor vaudeville houses and he is impressed with the opportunities offered to the American dramatist on those stages.

"The cast will be identical with that which is now presenting the play on the road, and differs very slightly from the one seen at the Herald Square Theatre, in this city, during the original run of the piece. Of course 'Mme. Butterfly' will be presented as only one feature of the Fifth Avenue's bill, which will retain unaltered its continuous vaudeville aspect.

"In addition to supervising the production of 'Mme. Butterfly,' Mr. Belasco has agreed with Mr. Proctor to furnish him and personally produce at least one other one-act play each season. These little plays will be toured over the Proctor circuit exclusively, the arrangement being to that effect. New scenery from the original models will be built for the Fifth Avenue production of 'Mme. Butterfly' and there will be some embellishment of the lighting effects, which were so impressive in the first run."

Mr. Belasco said last night: "I thoroughly believe in Mr. Proctor and his comprehensive and progressive ideas of vaudeville. He is daring, but shrewd; and I think he is going to cut a decided figure, not only in vaudeville, but in American theatricals generally. He made the proposition to me for the production of 'Mme. Butterfly' as a part of his Fifth

Avenue bill, and after considering the matter carefully I was not loath to make an engagement with him."

* * *

It was during the first decade of the new century that owners of rival circuits were watching Mr. Proctor's every move. It was practically impossible for him to hold an important conference in his office, in any other office or in a public hotel, for spotters were stationed in the various places around town frequented by theatre magnates and agents. So all conferences had to be held at his home in Larchmont or at his Central Valley estate, where he could have some privacy, usually on Sunday afternoons when he could give them undivided attention.

Jesse L. Lasky, one of Mr. Proctor's early collaborators, recalls such a visit.

His son, Fred, came to me at this time and said his dad would like me to visit him on Sunday afternoon at his home in Larchmont. I was happy to accept this invitation and spent the day with Mr. Proctor. He proved a most genial host and I soon discovered that his object in having me as his guest was to encourage me to produce more worthwhile attractions for vaudeville. He had real vision and emphasized again and again that unless more producers were recruited and encouraged to do the kind of attractions that I was doing, vaudeville would not survive.

This meeting so inspired me that for several years I devoted all my energies to producing numerous vaudeville attractions and the Proctor circuit was always the first to book them. Usually after I produced a new act, Mr. Proctor would drop me a line, generally praising the attraction. This generous action on his part was in contradiction to the usual attitude of the vaudeville magnates of that time, and was a distinguishing trait in Mr. Proctor's character. He was gentle and kind and extremely considerate, in striking contrast to the more hard-boiled showmen of his day.

* * *

The *New York World* of April 23, 1901, bore evidence of Mr. Proctor's constant fight to prevent vaudeville bills from becoming static or stale:

Having frowned upon the Association of Vaudeville Managers and divorced himself from it, Manager F. F. Proctor has also discarded at one of his houses the conventional form of continuous performance which it fostered.

At the Pleasure Palace yesterday he tried an experiment with a new kind of entertainment. With a fair cast he presented a play, preceded it with a curtain-raiser and filled in the intermissions between the acts with variety specialties. The result was a continuous entertainment more varied than he has given hitherto.

The play was the farce "Dr. Bill," and the curtain-raiser was Jerome K. Jerome's "Sunset." Both had been acted in New York before, but were new to the patrons of vaudeville theatres.

Among the specialty performers were Severus Schaeffer, the juggler; Press Eldridge, monologist, and Fritz, Leslie and Eddie, pantomimists.

* * *

A warm reminiscence of those wonderful days comes from the lovable Victor Moore:

The name of F. F. Proctor has always had a special meaning to me as it was in Proctor's 125th St. Theatre that "Change Your Act, or Back to the Woods" was first produced on July 2nd, 1902.

The skit, being a novelty and different from anything then in the variety theatres, attracted immediate attention and was a big hit from the start. The local manager called Mr. Proctor's attention to it and after seeing it himself immediately booked it in other Proctor houses, Newark, and the 5th Ave. being the only houses open at the time, but for years after it became "Vaudeville" the name of Moore & Littlefield headlined in all of the Proctor theatres.

In 1904 when he returned from a 4 weeks engagement in London we got off the boat on a Friday, and riding to our hotel we saw ourselves billed to open the following Monday in Proctor's 23rd St. Theatre, the date having been arranged by our agent while we were on the ocean.

Mr. Proctor was always cordial and helpful to all the acts that played in his theatres, and in theatres as well as in any other business the head of an organization generally reflects down through all employees, and in a Proctor theatre you were sure to find courteous, cheerful treatment from the manager to the stage door tender.

Vaudeville performers always had the most kindly feelings toward Mr. Proctor, whom they always considered a real benefactor, and a help to them in proper placement to best realize the value of their offerings.

Vaudeville during its popularity was a most satisfying form of entertainment, and together with the Keith and Orpheum circuits the Proctor houses were always a delight to play in.

Vaudeville can never come back, as it was essentially an intimate entertainment of personalities produced in small theatres, and in the big Picture theatres of today the Vaudeville bills as we knew them would be lost.

But any one who ever had any association with Mr. F. F. Proctor will always have the kindest thoughts of him and his treatment.

* * *

After 1900, it was a common experience to read newspaper stories reporting the construction of various Proctor theatres—always the handsomest in a given community. In 1905, he made another invasion of the Newark theatrical field by gaining three more important playhouses in that city, Proctor's Lyric Theatre (Market Street near Beaver Street), the Newark Bijou Dream Theatre (corner Washington Street and Branford Place), and Proctor's Palace Theatre and Proctor's Palace Roof Theatre (Market Street, between Halsey and Washington Streets).

This story, from the *New York Herald* of April 19, 1905, concerns the last of these three, and is uniform in pattern with many stories regarding the erection of Proctor theatres which were added to the circuit in the first quarter of the twentieth century:

A plot of ground with a frontage of 50 feet on Market Street, with an extension to Halsey Street, Newark, has been purchased by F. F. Proctor, the New York theatrical man, who will at once begin the erection of a theatre and roof garden on the site. The theatre, the plans for which have already been drawn, will be the largest in the city, and the roof garden will compare favorably with anything in New York.

It is said that the new venture means an outlay of $1,000,000. The site is within a block and a half of the "Four Corners," the principal square in the city.

(END OF ACT 3)

ACT FOUR

Building the Big Time

By 1900 the Proctor theatrical empire was established so solidly that its ruler was able to devote his time and energy to the improvement of the arts which were the lifeblood of his enterprises. He saw clearly that the building of big-time vaudeville was his special province. A small item on the theatrical page of the *New York World* on April 14, 1900, hints the greatness that was coming.

> Thomas Q. Seabrooke has been engaged at a salary of $1,000 a week by F. F. Proctor to open the Fifth Avenue Theatre as his third vaudeville house in New York. The opening will take place three weeks from next Monday. Until then Joseph Jefferson will hold the boards, beginning Monday.

The *New York Herald* of September 9, 1901, tells of Proctor's engagement of Eugene Sandow, the famous strong man, and of many other well-known European vaudeville performers. Sandow in November of the same year had a special audience with President Theodore Roosevelt in the White House, and later he became adviser on physical fitness to Presidents Roosevelt and Taft and was said to have made over $50,000 a year. His reported engagement to Lillian Russell gave New York a subject for conversation for many months.

The *New York Morning Telegraph* of Sept. 10, 1902, announced:

> Among the plans outlined by F. F. Proctor yesterday for the current season is the announcement that Minnie Seligman has been engaged as

leading woman at the Fifth Avenue Theatre, beginning there next Monday afternoon in "The Great Ruby."

Miss Seligman will take the part of the adventuress, Countess Mirza, while James E. Wilson, the new leading man, who was formerly at the American, will also have a prominent role.

The press agent was busy yesterday telling of Miss Seligman's wonderful new gowns, and her equally wonderful salary (the greatest ever). But more interesting than these details is the statement that she will presently masquerade as the girl-boy Rosalind in Shakespeare's "As You Like It," and there will be at least six novel and important productions in the course of the season. Manuscript plays by prominent dramatists are now being read with a view to a proper selection.

The stock system will be continued also at Proctor's Fifty-eighth Street and 125th Street houses. At Fifty-eighth Street, melodrama will be the principal offering, with Harrison J. Wolfe and Edna Archer Crawford as the chief players. At 125th Street both melodrama and farce will be presented, with Adelaide Keim and Ned Howard Fowler at the head of the company.

The Twenty-third Street Proctor House will give continuous vaudeville, while the Albany and Montreal theatres will duplicate the Fifth Avenue productions each week.

Proctor now controls five permanently located stock companies, employing more people than any other stock manager, as well as two theatres devoted exclusively to continuous vaudeville. The new addition to the Fifth Avenue lobby will be thrown open within a month.

Mr. Fynes* refused to pointedly deny the frequently recurring rumor that Mr. Proctor intends to extend his circuit so as to include Boston and Philadelphia in which cities B. F. Keith is now holding sway in the line of popular-priced amusements. Mr. Fynes said: "The indefinite extension of Mr. Proctor's circuit is simply a matter of his personal inclination. What the next few months may bring forth I do not care to state just now."

* * *

* J. Austin Fynes, long associated with Mr. Proctor, had previously been a rival as manager of Keith's Union Square Theatre and had attempted to outbid him in hiring stars for variety performances.

The Proctor organization put out only three promotion booklets in its entire fifty years' history. The first of the trio in 1902 described the entire Proctor system at that time.

Distributed throughout this 1902 booklet were pictures of these Proctor performers: Bessie Barriscale, Frederic Bond, Mrs. Eva Vincent, Sumner Gard, Adelaide Keim, Hudson Liston, Charles M. Seay, Edna Archer Crawford, Richard Lyle, James Castle, Beatrice Morgan, Julian Reed, Sol Aiden, Mabel Montgomery, Wallace Erskine, William Gerald, Florence Leslie, George Friend, Ada Levick, Frederick Truesdell and Adeline Raffetto.

Interspersed among these pictures was the following text:

On April 22, 1901, at the Fifty-eighth Street Theatre, Mr. Proctor introduced to his patrons the F. F. Proctor Big Stock Co. The venture, which was purely experimental, was instantaneously successful. The number of companies was increased week by week until there were six separate branches of the organization. Never in the history of theatricals had an itinerant stock of such magnitude been conducted. During the year which has elapsed more than five hundred different players have found employment in Mr. Proctor's service; more than two hundred and fifty comedies and over one hundred curtain raisers have been presented. The expense of making scenic productions of each presentation has been enormous, but the generous support and enthusiastic plaudits of the public have spurred the management to restless energy. Reward for careful attention to every detail has come not alone in unparalleled financial returns but in the generous praise of the press and the comments of patrons.

* * *

Mr. Proctor intends to maintain his record of providing the latest plays, interpreted by the most skillful players, equipped with adequate scenic effects and costumed elaborately. Everything that years of experience can bring to bear; all that money can secure and ambition can produce will be centralized in the entertainments presented by the

F. F. Proctor Stock Co. in the future, with a firm determination to outstrip the splendid record of the past.

* * *

Sunday concerts are given at the four Proctor theatres in New York, beginning at 2 o'clock P. M. and running continuously afternoon and evening. Vaudeville specialists whose offerings are in keeping with the character of the day are specially engaged to augment the variety numbers which claim attention on week days at the various theatres. For the Sunday concerts there is no increase in the popular scale of prices, and yet the entertainments are admittedly the best to be seen anywhere in the city.

Dainty souvenirs are given to the ladies in attendance upon the daily matinees at the One Hundred and Twenty-fifth St., Fifty-eighth St. and Proctor's Newark Theatres. These mementos are selected with a special view to attracting and pleasing the lady patrons, and suggestions for appropriate tokens are invited. Suitable prizes are offered, and many excellent ideas have been advanced. These will be acted upon in due season, and the plan of distributing souvenirs every afternoon at the theatres named will probably be continued indefinitely.

* * *

A few of the best seats on the orchestra floor—the first few front rows—are reserved, numbered coupon tickets for which may be secured a week in advance of the date upon which it is the intention to use them. The plan was recently put in operation at the request of hosts of patrons, and is a success.

* * *

The Twenty-third Street Theatre was New York's first home of continuous vaudeville. The policy of presenting the best acts procurable still obtains. Attractions from the European music halls and the leading American artists are weekly presented. The leading stars in the variety profession are seen first in this theatre. There is the same degree of care displayed in presenting the vaudeville bills at the Twenty-third Street that marks the productions by the F. F. Proctor Big Stock Co. at the other six theatres on the Proctor Circuit. Performances begin at noon and continue uninterruptedly until nearly midnight. There are always diversity and merit in the Proctor vaudevilles; always quantity in abundance and quality unsurpassed; but, above all, refinement has predominating sway.

* * *

The Proctor Entertainments

"The Play's The Thing—With A Little Good Vaudeville" is doubtless the way Shakespeare would have written it had Mr. Proctor been conducting a theatre in Stratford-on-Avon at the time "Hamlet" was written. The idea of interlarding the best acts in vaudeville with dramatic presentations, combining the whole in continuous performance, is original with Mr. Proctor. Others have experimented in a small way, and many have copied his ideas, but it is in his theatres alone that the best exemplification of the new departure is to be witnessed. By this method there is entertainment for both the vaudeville devotee and the patron of the drama. Both branches are conducted independently, but are nevertheless allied artistically in one grand continuous performance. By the introduction of vaudeville between the acts the long and tedious waits usually attendant upon the setting of the stage for a succeeding act of the drama is obviated. There is something to entertain and amuse ALL the time; and there are no dull moments in an afternoon or evening spent at Proctor's.

* * *

Full orchestras were recently established at the Fifth Avenue, the One Hundred and Twenty-fifth and the Fifty-eighth Street Theatres. The new departure has been immensely popular from the very outset. Programmes of classical and popular selections are artistically blended, and skillful musicians, under the baton of most competent leaders, serve to agreeably augment the stage performance. "Request" numbers are a popular feature, and most of the selections are made in compliance with the wishes of patrons, providing, of course, that they are in keep-

BUILDING THE BIG TIME 77

ing with the artistic purpose of the managerial desire to furnish up-to-date programmes.

* * *

Four theatres in New York, one in Newark, one in Albany and one in Montreal make up the Proctor Circuit of seven beautiful playhouses devoted to the purpose of providing refined entertainments for the multitude. This is the largest chain of theatres under the sole control and individual ownership of one person in the world. To properly conduct these theatres, equip them with weekly changes of bill and maintain Mr. Proctor's long established reputation for refined, wholesome and worthy entertainment requires no small degree of managerial acumen and capacity for incessant and skillful work.

* * *

Playing to thousands upon thousands of people annually, the Proctor Theatres are able to present better entertainments at lower admission rates than any other playhouses in America. Pennies count quickly into dollars when they pour into one coffer from several sources. The same pocketbook bears the burden of salaries, and the individual Proctor patron reaps the benefit of better entertainment because of the several theatres under Mr. Proctor's ownership. It is a simple proposition of buying talent at wholesale and distributing it at retail. Because of the number of weeks he can offer the vaudeville artist or the player Mr. Proctor is able to negotiate advantageously.

* * *

Every play which is produced by the F. F. Proctor Big Stock Co. is mounted with special scenic effects. The Proctor Scenic Studio is indeed a hive of industry. To properly equip each play, with the weekly changes of bill in each theatre, requires a large force of expert and experienced artisans. Once in a while the original scenery is used; but in such cases the plot of the play hinges upon mechanical effects which it is impractical and unnecessary to produce. New scenery, new costumes and special lighting effects are the most important details of the perfect productions which have won fame and favor for the Proctor players. The comedies presented are from the pens of the best American and foreign authors. The manner of their presentation is in many instances superior to the original.

* * *

Laughter is Nature's most potent panacea for all the depressing moods flesh is heir to. Use your wealth to benefit your health and visit Proctor's. Bring your most critical mood with you—we know our plays and players will stand the severest test. Enterprise is the vital force in amusement methods, and the Proctor entertainments have stood the test of criticism with marked success. Anyone who is short on coin and long on "the blues" will find agreeable conditions and a pleasant atmosphere at Proctor's. There is always plenty of laughter, pretty women, fine scenery, gorgeous costumes, good music, comfortable chairs, polite attention, and all one has to do is to go ahead and enjoy themselves. The Proctor bills make life easy for the woebegone, and shed cheer upon the pathway of the troubled mortal.

* * *

Mr. Proctor was the pioneer of popular prices. It was he who originated the low scale of theatrical admission rates, which at one time amounted to a popular craze. Even now scores of managers are enriching themselves at the original "Proctor Prices" of admissions. In conducting his various theatres, Mr. Proctor looks first to the financial capacity of the multitudes, and his prices—25, 35 and 50 cents—include a fit for every purse. There are reserved seats for 75 cents and box seats for $1, to accommodate those who are willing to pay a slightly increased rate for the privilege of reserving their locations in advance.

* * *

Proctor's Theatre, Newark, the latest addition to the Proctor Circuit, is admittedly the handsomest theatre in America devoted exclusively to vaudeville. Opened on January 6, of the present year, the season has thus far been phenomenally successful, crowds thronging the theatre at both daily performances. Refined vaudeville is presented in the same skillful manner in which all of the Proctor entertainments are conducted. The daily bargain matinees, when 25 cents admits to all orchestra or balcony seats, are crowded with ladies. The location of the theatre, fronting on Military Park, is in the very heart of the shopping district, making it easy of access.

* * *

It is a fact that the press is largely instrumental in the success or failure of theatrical enterprises. Where meritorious entertainments are put forward, the news is disseminated in the public prints, and when unworthy offerings are made the information is as promptly known. Mr. Proctor returns thanks to the press for favors.

* * *

Uniformed Superintendents, ushers and attaches pay careful attention to the wants of patrons at all Proctor's theatres. Matrons are in charge of the ladies' retiring rooms, and there are check rooms for the reception of parcels. Politeness is exacted from all who wear the Proctor regalia. The Superintendents are responsible for all employees, and complaints of incivility upon the part of any attache should be made to the Superintendent, who will immediately investigate. All attaches of the Proctor theatres are experienced in their several callings. The stage is in charge of competent managers, and the entertainments are carefully supervised and censored.

The Sunday Concerts mentioned in this Proctor pamphlet were the ingenious invention of Proctor and others to replace vaudeville which had been prohibited in New York by a recent "blue law."

In 1904, Proctor's hunt for outstanding talent was in full swing. On May 13th, readers of the *New York World* were informed of one of its great finds:

The beckoning fingers of vaudeville and the purse-strings they control have lured Charles Hawtrey, one of the best actors from England, out of the narrow path of the "legitimate" into the broad-gauged track of specialty "artists," song-and-dance teams and acrobatic experts.

Manager F. F. Proctor, who controls four vaudeville houses in New York, made the announcement yesterday that he had engaged

Mr. Hawtrey for next week and that he would appear four times daily at two of his theatres—the Twenty-third street house and the Fifth Avenue Theatre.

The salary which the actor will receive for this foray into varieties is not stated, but it is said to be exceptional. All managers admit that it is the greatest coup yet made by an ambitious vaudeville manager.

Mr. Hawtrey will act in a sketch by Mrs. Ruth Bell and Arthur Cecil, entitled "Time Is Money." It is a comedietta in which he once appeared in London and the time of its performance is about thirty minutes.

The sketch will go on at Proctor's Twenty-third Street Theatre at 3 o'clock in the afternoon and at 9 o'clock in the evening. At the conclusion of each performance Mr. Hawtrey will jump into a cab and be driven six blocks to the Fifth Avenue Theatre, where he will act it again with a duplicate suite of scenery.

Among Mr. Hawtrey's confreres in the Proctor vaudeville performance will be a "facial contortionist," a "premiere bicycle team," a "black-face artist," and a knockabout act, moving pictures and several comedy sketches.

The following week Mr. Hawtrey will sail for England.

Manager Proctor sold yesterday his Montreal theatre to the J. B. Sparrow Amusement Company of Montreal. This house was located too far from the Proctor circuit.

* * *

May Robson, one of the greatest character actresses of the twentieth century, was the next star to appear at the Proctor theatres. In September 1904 she played a Cockney slavey in "Cinders," a one-act comedy.

Even more grandiose plans were made before the year 1904 was over, though Mr. Proctor could not then carry them out. The *New York Morning Telegraph* of November 23, 1904, printed the following:

The formation of a new vaudeville circuit, embracing a chain of houses in the leading cities from coast to coast, is the news that comes

The Four Cohans, long Friends of the Proctors

George M. Cohan

PROCTOR'S FIFTH AVENUE

Vaudeville's Greatest Capture.

IT is with sincere pleasure that MR. F. F. PROCTOR announces that he has effected what is conceded to be the most brilliant and important engagement in the history of vaudeville. "In securing

MISS LILLIAN RUSSELL

for his theatres, MR. PROCTOR," says The Press, "has simply amazed this public by his daring and liberal enterprise. Her beauty and her thoroughly artistic talent will make the appearance of this famous prima-donna on the PROCTOR stage an event long to be remembered by patrons of 'all-star vaudeville.'"

MR. PROCTOR begs to announce that the engagement of MISS RUSSELL will be inaugurated on

MONDAY, OCTOBER 2 Next,

AT

PROCTOR'S 23d Street,

where the famous American beauty and prima-donna will be heard every afternoon and evening (including Sundays) for a period of indefinite length. She will present during her engagement a repertory of her most famous songs, as well as a number of new selections, and she will make her debut memorable by wearing some of the most beautiful creations of the modiste's art ever displayed on any stage.

☞ Seats for any afternoon or night of Miss Russell's engagement will be reserved on application at the Box Office.

LILLIAN RUSSELL HANDBILL

THEATRE MANAGERS

DANIEL FROHMAN
MANAGER
LYCEUM THEATRE

MAURICE GRAU
ABBEY, SCHÖFFEL & GRAU
OPERA AND THEATRICAL MANAGERS

AL. HAYMAN
THEATRICAL MANAGER
KNICKERBOCKER THEATRE, NEW YORK

FREDERICK FREEMAN PROCTOR
PROPRIETOR AND MANAGER
PROCTOR'S THEATRE, PROCTOR'S PLEASURE PALACE

KING'S NOTABLE NEW YORKERS

THEATRE PROPRIETORS

BENJAMIN FRANKLIN KEITH
KEITH'S UNION SQUARE THEATRE, NEW YORK
KEITH'S THEATRES, BOSTON, PHILA., PROVIDENCE, ETC.

HENRY CLAY MINER
PROP. 5TH AVE., PEOPLE'S AND 8TH AVE. THEATRES IN N. Y.
AND MINER'S THEATRE, NEWARK. U. S. CONGRESS (1895-97)

GUSTAV AMBERG
DIRECTOR AND FOUNDER
AMBERG'S (NOW IRVING PLACE) THEATRE

ANTONIO PASTOR
ACTOR AND THEATRICAL MANAGER
FOUNDER TONY PASTOR'S THEATRE

NELLIE LINGARD, GEORGIE'S COUSIN, DAUGHTER OF JAMES W. LINGARD, IN "TESS OF THE D'URBERVILLES"

by wire from Chicago, right on the heels of F. F. Proctor's return yesterday from an extended business tour through the middle West.

Mr. Proctor's Napoleonic achievement is the arrangement of a combination with the Hyde & Behman and other vaudeville interests, by which performers will get seventeen weeks' time in all the large cities between New York and Chicago; and a further stroke of policy in forming a coalition with the Western Orpheum circuit, through which it will be possible to book performers from coast to coast, and for a season of fifty-two weeks, if they so desire.

This will be great news for the distracted vaudeville performers, whose dates have recently gone all awry through managerial bickerings.

Mr. Proctor did not come back to New York to announce his business triumphs with a flourish of trumpets. He kept his counsel and could not be reached to give confirmation to the report of the deal, which had already been affirmed by his new business colleagues.

The new plan will go into effect January 1, according to dispatches from Chicago. So far as outlined, it embraces an arrangement of existing vaudeville circuits covering seventeen vaudeville theatres in New York, Brooklyn, Newark, Jersey City, Philadelphia, Baltimore, Pittsburgh, Chicago and other cities not named. So far as perfected, the plan contemplates giving performers the option of playing twice each season over this circuit.

As it stands, the arrangement is a practical Proctor-Hyde & Behman combination.

The other details which dovetail into these are the formation of a coalition with the Western vaudeville circuit controlling the Orpheum houses in such a way that it will be possible to have a complete transcontinental circuit that would be of infinite value. In this connection a report has come from San Francisco to the effect that an attempt is being made there to combine the Orpheum circuit with a certain Eastern circuit (unnamed), so as to get the complete fifty-two weeks of the year into one booking.

To Destroy All Friction

This later report goes on to state that S. H. Friedlander is to be the Eastern representative, with headquarters in the New York Theatre

Building, and the telegram from Chicago says that Paige Smith is to be sent to Europe to look after the new interests there. It is also announced that under no circumstances will the Music Hall in Chicago be turned back into the dramatic line again. It will remain irrevocably a vaudeville theatre, and will naturally form a part of the new arrangement.

If this arrangement is an accomplished fact, which there seems no reason to doubt, there is absolutely no chance that any friction will arise, and the indications are that the vaudeville field will be divided pretty evenly in this country, both organizations working without any of the bitterness that characterized the business a few years ago, prior to the formation of the Vaudeville Managers' Association, which is now upon its last legs. As a matter of interest, it may be stated that the Managers' Association was only contracted for a term of five years, and this term expires about May 1, 1905.

The importance of such an arrangement, which lacks only the confirmation of Mr. Proctor, to the performer is enormous. Not only will an act of merit be booked for a complete tour of as many weeks as the performer cares to play, but this route will take in every section of the country, from Maine to California, and from Canada to the Mexican border.

In this connection it may also be noted that within the past week a combination of Southern managers has been effected in such a manner as to insure some proper working in a systematic way of the various opposing interests of the South.

During recent years there have been countless rumors of impending warfare in the vaudeville ranks, and certain individuals connected in a more or less haphazard way with the business have taken it upon themselves to prophesy the bitterest kind of a fight.

The only thing that takes the edge off such rumors as these is the fact that the wars never take place, and that any combination of interests always has been effected in a quiet and thoroughly amicable manner for the best interests of all concerned.

Mr. Proctor was years ahead of his time when his idea for "a great vaudeville amalgamation to extend from the Atlantic to the Pacific" was publicized, for example, in the *New York Morning Telegraph* of November 28, 1904, as follows:

(Special Dispatch to *The Morning Telegraph*)

PITTSBURGH, Nov. 27.

Despite denials from New York, Manager Harry Davis, of this city, still is sponsor for the statement that F. F. Proctor has in mind a great vaudeville amalgamation, to extend from the Atlantic to the Pacific, with the Hyde & Behman interests as an important factor. Mr. Proctor, by the way, was in conference with Mr. Davis here during the week. The latter said today:

"Mr. Proctor's plan is not a new one. It was broached a number of years ago, but fell through. It looks as if something now may be accomplished. The project is to organize a central booking agency for leading theatres, using stock plays. The same agency could engage costumes and scenery, and pay royalties on the plays. The central agency would be a sort of mutual affair, and not a money-making concern.

"The managers of the stock houses now carry on correspondence with owners of plays, which is slow and expensive. Oftentimes we are held off so long that we do not have enough time to finish painting scenery and for the actors to learn their lines. Mr. Proctor's idea is to secure the original scenery whenever possible, especially in large productions. By using a play one or more weeks in New York and other Eastern cities, the scenery and costumes can be shipped West.

"It is the intention, if possible, to organize a circuit, so a play can be produced at a string of theatres to the Pacific Coast, and, by taking another route, the same play can be presented at enough towns to more than pay the expenses back to the starting point again.

Working on Proper Lines

"In this manner, the stage managers would be relieved of much hard work and the expenses would be reduced materially to every stock house in the country. I do not know positively whether Mr. Proctor can persuade enough theatre owners to go in with him, but he is working along the proper lines."

Mr. Proctor while here expressed himself to theatrical men as in favor of erecting several new theatres. He was impressed with the style of architecture adopted by Architect Marshall in the Nixon Theatre, and he proposes to erect a similar house somewhere in the West.

* * *

Though these plans for a coast-to-coast organization did not go through, Mr. Proctor was as active as ever in getting new talent. On March 9, 1905, the *New York World* carried this item.

Mme. Yvette Guilbert, the noted French singer and comedienne who was brought to this country a few weeks ago by Charles Frohman and who announced her last New York chanson recital last night at the Lyceum Theatre, has suddenly signed a contract with F. F. Proctor whereby she is to appear for four weeks in his vaudeville theatres.

At least a dozen vaudeville managers have been eager to engage Mme. Guilbert since she stepped off the steamer, yet she refused to entertain the idea of a variety engagement. But Mr. Proctor made her an offer which she could not resist. The figure is not announced, but the manager said last night that he would pay the comedienne considerably more than he did Lillian Russell.

Mme. Guilbert will finish her tour of the principal cities under Mr. Frohman's management in two weeks. Then she will return to New York and appear on Easter Monday at Proctor's Twenty-third Street Theatre, after which she will be seen at the Fifty-eighth street house and possibly at the Fifth Avenue Theatre.

In addition to her "Chansons Pompadour" and "Chansons Crinoline" Mme. Guilbert will render English songs. The latter may include several which brought her fame when she appeared some years ago at Koster & Bial's Music-Hall.

* * *

Even the most imaginative rival manager would not have suspected Mr. Proctor of his next two moves—the capture of the two Lilys—Langtry and Russell! These two coups were announced within ten days in June 1905. The *World* for the 18th had the Langtry story.

Lily Langtry is to appear in New York in vaudeville for ten weeks this fall.

The Jersey Lily clinched a bargain by cable last night, and the salary she is to receive is said to be the largest for such a period ever paid by American or European managers.

She is to receive $2,500 a week, or $25,000 for ten weeks, after which she is to return to London and go on with her own remodelling of Pinero's play "Iris."

It took the united nerve of three American managers to propose vaudeville to Lily Langtry. The three are Oscar Hammerstein, F. F. Proctor and Percy G. Williams, who, with the Keiths are the biggest dispensers of continuous performance and vaudeville in this country.

The suggestion came from the other side. The Jersey Lily, who has always devoted her talents to brisk legitimate in the drama, returned from South Africa a few weeks ago and began on Pinero's "Iris" to make something out of it more to her own taste. She plans to produce it in the fall London season.

The managers of the London Coliseum stepped forward with a vaudeville offer of $1,250 a week for a few weeks in the summer. This was heard on this side of the water, with the result of setting the three heads of the American managers together. They began cable negotiations last week. They did not say if it took much coaxing to bring the Jersey Lily to vaudeville.

The plan is to have her appear under the management of Oscar Hammerstein for two weeks, Proctor for four weeks and Percy Williams for three weeks. During the remaining week of the contract she will appear in Boston or some other Eastern city under joint management.

"Will she do a monologue stunt?" a wag asked the three last night.

"She will do a monologue," replied the managers in all seriousness. "At least that is the plan now, or we may decide to put her in a short play with American support."

* * *

And then, only nine days later, on the 27th, the same paper printed this story about Lillian Russell.

It became known yesterday that F. F. Proctor, the vaudeville manager, is making a strenuous attempt to add Miss Lillian Russell to the list of his stars. Three months ago negotiations were opened, and an offer was made by the theatrical manager on a basis of $2,000 a week salary for a season of thirty weeks. The singer refused and demanded double the sum. Whereupon Manager Proctor proposed a compromise at $3,000 a week.

J. Austin Fynes, general manager for Mr. Proctor, said yesterday that no contract had been made as yet, but that the prima donna was considering the offer. If she agreed, he said, she would appear in songs from famous operas and her costumes would dazzle audiences.

* * *

About a month later the *World* definitely announced that Miss Russell had signed up with Proctor. Here is part of the *World's* August 1, 1905, story.

Lillian Russell is at last going into vaudeville. In Saratoga yesterday afternoon she signed a contract with F. F. Proctor to appear under Mr. Proctor's direction for an indefinite period.

She will make her vaudeville debut at the manager's Twenty-third Street Theatre early in October, and will sing every afternoon and evening, including Sundays, throughout her engagement. Miss Russell will remain at the Twenty-third Street Theatre as many weeks as may be warranted by the conditions of business. She will then appear at Mr. Proctor's other theatres.

Miss Russell may also make a tour of the larger cities under Mr. Proctor's management.

* * *

About this time Eugene K. Allen closed a lengthy editorial on Mr. Proctor and his career with the startling facts and figures of the contract. For two performances daily (including Sundays) Lillian Russell got a 33-week contract calling for payment of $100,000!

Diamond Jim Brady bought a box for the entire duration of Lillian Russell's engagement (5 weeks) at Proctor's Twenty-third Street Theatre. After she finished her act each night, he waited for her and they would drive away from the theatre together.

The following paragraphs, quoted from *Lillian Russell, The Era of Plush,* are reprinted by courtesy of Random House, Inc.:

During her annual visit to Saratoga in the summer of 1905, Lillian had held an enlightening and profitable conversation with F. F. Proctor, the vaudeville magnate. Variety had come a long way from the music halls of the Sixties and Seventies and the pioneer efforts of Tony Pastor. Now it ranked just behind the musical shows in lavishness and popularity. All vaudeville needed, Proctor cannily told Lillian, was the patronage of a great star like herself to bestow upon it the final dignity and authority of a really legitimate branch of the theatre.

Lillian listened graciously, but refused to commit herself at the moment. To enter vaudeville was a big step for any star of her caliber to take, and, to some degree, a desperate one.

If she *should* accept Proctor's offer—and, mind you, she made it clear, it was not at all definite that she would—it must necessarily be at a very high salary.

All this could be arranged satisfactorily, the variety man assured her. His theatres had a far greater capacity, in most cases, than the Broadway houses, and this alone, plus the fact that there would be two shows a day, including Sundays, could more than enable him to meet her demands.

Lillian pondered a few more days and presently met Proctor with new questions. Could he assure her that she would be presented in a manner quite in keeping with the greatness of her reputation? How many songs would she have to sing at each performance? What about the musical director? Would she have to be dependent upon the vagaries of the house orchestra leader in each vaudeville theatre where she appeared?

Everything could be arranged, Mr. Proctor reiterated. It was entirely to his own advantage, he hastened to point out, to present her in as dignified and dramatic a way as possible. She need sing no more than three songs at each performance, but it was imperative that she adorn herself to the hilt.

"The men won't care so much about this part of the act," Proctor reminded her, "but the women will. They will insist upon seeing Lillian Russell in the latest styles from Paris, the most modern coiffure and wearing all her jewels."

All *that* could be easily taken care of, Lillian reminded the impresario somewhat frostily. In matters sartorial she had never let her public down yet, and vaudeville certainly could depend upon her to maintain her own tradition.

The other details were quickly and easily arranged. Lillian was to have her own orchestra leader and pianist who would go with her to every theatre she played. There would even be an auction sale of seats and boxes for her opening matinee and evening performances. And, what was even more important, there would be a contract for ten weeks at $3,000 a week.

Under the circumstances, it would have been folly to refuse an offer like this, and Lillian needed no maxim from the writings of Marcus Aurelius to tell her so. She signed the contract with a jubilation that she took no trouble to conceal.

Her opening, on October 2nd, at Proctor's 23rd Street Theatre was celebrated with the pomp and pageantry accorded royalty. In order that Lillian might not have to risk the ruin of her elaborate gowns by walking up and down the iron stairs that led to the dressing rooms, a special property room to the left of the stage was cleared of its contents and elaborately re-decorated with silk and satin hangings and eight full-length pier glasses. Even the stage and its approaches had not been neglected, for here was a rich, wide carpet laid down to protect her clothing from the dust and splinters.

Further to dignify the occasion, nearly every first-string drama critic in town attended the opening performance. Their reviews next day were somewhat perplexed. Acton Davies, of the *Sun*, reported that it was difficult to decide who was the more nervous at first, Lillian or the audience. No one seemed to know quite what to do about it all. The cash customers obviously regarded Lillian as an old curiosity who must prove her value—a challenge to which the singer was more than equal. By the time she had finished singing "Napoli" by Edwards, and "Your Kiss" by Louis Gottschalk, there wasn't an apathetic listener in the house. The Russell magnetism had lost none of its power. Lillian seemed to reach out over the footlights and attract everyone into her embrace.

"Songs may come and songs may go," Davies concluded, "but age cannot wither nor variety custom stale Miss Russell. She is the same old Lillian, and her voice is the same old voice. . . ."

On December 16th, having successfully finished one of the most profitable engagements in her long and varied career, Lillian sailed for Europe aboard the *Kaiser Wilhelm*. She planned, it was said, to see what possibilities there were of picking up a successful European musical show for her next season. Actually, she had a much more practical mission than this. In Paris, she would buy several trunkloads of the most elaborate dresses she could find, and later, upon her return, would again dazzle the patrons of vaudeville.

Late in March she returned to America, and, on April 16th, opened a vaudeville engagement in Brooklyn. This tour, which lasted six weeks, was in every sense as successful as the first, yet, such is the perversity of queens and actresses, when F. F. Proctor approached her about signing for a third engagement, Lillian refused.

Miss Russell realized her voice would one day fail her and that if she were to continue as a public entertainer it would have to be in some other way. And she believed she had found the answer—*acting*! Consequently, she had her mind and eye on the dramatic field, as separate and distinct from vaudeville.

* * *

It was one of Mr. Proctor's ambitions to make special use of the scores of stars he had under contract to give the patrons of his Fifth Avenue Theatre at new low prices plays as good as any that Broadway playgoers had ever seen. The *New York World* of June 28, 1905, printed this article:

Theatre-goers who are on the lookout for new plays performed by competent actors at rates cheaper than those now charged by first-class Broadway theatres will find them in plenty after Sept. 1 at the Fifth Avenue Theatre, where a complete change of policy will be made by Manager F. F. Proctor.

For some time the head of the Proctor interests in New York has been engaging actors of reputation and ability. He intends to assemble them in a strong stock organization, which is to be made a permanent feature at the Fifth Avenue Theatre, when the present two-performances-a-day system will be discarded, the rates raised to $1.50 for best seats and a regular stock company season instituted.

Mr. Proctor's present list of prominent players already includes Henry Miller, Harry Woodruff, Minnie Seligman, Annie Irish and Elita Proctor Otis. To these many others will be added.

* * *

Many pages of this book could be filled with excited contemporary newspaper comment on Mr. Proctor's coups, rumored or actual. Perhaps it will suffice to summarize a few of these, giving names of newspapers and dates of issue for the source.

In July 1905 (New York *Morning Telegraph*, 27th) Mr. Proctor announced that he had signed Amelia Bingham and Charles Richman—who both had previous plans for starring tours for the season—for his Fifth Avenue Theatre, with Gertrude Coghlan to play ingenue leads.

Then in September 1905 (*Morning Telegraph*, 3rd) theatre-goers heard that the all-star Fifth Avenue stock company would include—besides Miss Bingham, Charles Richman and Gertrude Coghlan—J. H. Gilmour, Charles Dickson, Louise Allen Collier, Florence Rockewell, Charles Abbe, Gerald Steen, Harold Hartsell and Adeline Wesley. Among the plays promised were "The Frisky Mrs. Johnson," "The Climbers" and "The Sporting Duchess."

In March 1906 (New York *Tribune*, 2nd; Hartford *Courant*, 5th) or just before that time Mr. Proctor offered Mme. Calvé

$20,000 a week for two weeks, to sing twice a day, two songs in the afternoon and two at night, each appearance lasting only ten minutes. But she refused and sailed away to France.

And the same month (*New York World*, March 15th) Mr. Proctor offered and Anna Held refused $10,000 for four weeks on the Proctor circuit.

The Fifth Avenue and the other New York City theatres, of course, were increasingly important in these plans of Mr. Proctor, but the following paragraphs from a long news story in the *Morning Telegraph* for September 3rd, 1905, about the Proctor interests show how strong they were outside the metropolitan area.

At the Newark theatre vaudeville has never been interfered with, and the theatre will be continued along that line, for it would be the height of folly to disturb what is one of the best paying investments in that city.

Albany will also continue with all star vaudeville throughout the coming Winter season, although the stock company will be restored next Summer, as it has been found to be the most popular hot weather entertainment. The new theatre Mr. Proctor has obtained in Troy will be opened to the public next Monday and the policy will be similar to that in Albany.

Taken altogether, Mr. Proctor is looming up on the dramatic horizon as one of the most enterprising of managers and the continuation of his present policy seems to spell success. Among the many vaudeville features engaged by him for the season, in addition to Miss Russell, are Katie Barry, James J. Corbett, Carmencita, Rice & Prevost, Adele Ritchie, Harry Gilfoil, Abdul Kader, Rossi's Musical Horse, the Hengler Sisters, Valerie Bergere, Papinta, Nella Bergen and several of the best artists of the London and Parisian music halls.

* * *

Interesting comment on Mr. Proctor's activities at this point in his career was published in *Leslie's Magazine*, issue of September 23, 1905.

F. F. PROCTOR

In the dramatic news of the day, no one occupies a position to which so much interest attaches just now as Mr. Frederick Freeman Proctor, the progressive and daring impresario, who finds even the queenly and hitherto prohibitive-priced Lillian Russell within his reach for vaudeville, and who has organized and is presenting the first real all-star stock company New York has known for many years. Mr. Proctor is a native of Dexter, Me., and recently celebrated his fiftieth birthday. He is the son of a physician, who placed him as a boy in a Young Men's Christian Association gymnasium of Boston, where he early acquired a knowledge of and fondness for acrobatic work. He left the dry-goods house in which he was employed and entered the amusement field as one of the afterward celebrated Levantine Brothers. He has been a manager for thirty years, and now owns four theatres in New York, one in Albany, one in Troy, and one in Newark. At one time he had an interest in twenty-one. It was he who gave Mr. Charles Frohman his first dramatic home in this city, and Klaw & Erlanger owe their first New York roof to him. He established vaudeville in the metropolis and originated the continuous show here. Mr. Proctor has a palatial town house in West Thirty-fourth Street, and a fine country residence at Larchmont Manor, where he is still known as one of the most powerful swimmers in the settlement. He has two married daughters and one son, Frederick F. Proctor, Jr., who takes an active interest in all of his father's business enterprises. Mr. Proctor's real-estate holdings are extensive. He has great faith in that form of investment, and is now building in Albany the first large modern apartment-house in that city.

* * *

The second of the three promotion pamphlets to which the Proctor organization confined its booklet publishing activity was issued in 1906, on the occasion of Mr. Proctor's twenty-fifth anniversary as a showman. It was another unpretentious souvenir measuring 5 inches by 7 inches and containing 16 pages. The cover bore a portrait of Mr. Proctor, above which appeared the following title:

F. F. PROCTOR'S
TWENTY-FIFTH ANNIVERSARY JUBILEE
CELEBRATED *at* PROCTOR'S FIFTH AVENUE THEATRE
The WEEK *of* APRIL NINTH, NINETEEN HUNDRED *and* SIX

This booklet contained full-page portraits and biographies of six stars—Henri de Vries, Mabel Taliaferro, Le Domino Rouge, Vesta Victoria, Mme. Yvette Guilbert and Fred Walton. It carried vignettes of Amelia Bingham, A. H. Van Buren, H. Dudley Hawley, James J. Corbett, Isabelle Evesson and James Young. Also included were scenes from the following plays: "If I Were King," "Mrs. Jack," "Mlle. Marni," "Mr. Smooth," "Candida," and "The Merchant of Venice."

The last three pages contained the following material about the Proctor Circuit theatres generally and Proctor's Fifth Avenue Theatre in particular.

Mr. F. F. Proctor's Enterprises

Proctor's Fifth Avenue Theatre
    Located on the corner of Broadway and Twenty-eighth street and devoted to the presentation of a dramatic production, with change of bill weekly, by an All-Star Company of Players.

Proctor's Twenty-third Street Theatre
    Located on Twenty-third street, just west of Sixth avenue, and considered the leading vaudeville theatre in America. This playhouse has been famous as the "Home of Novelty," as its programmes are the most varied and original in New York.

Proctor's Fifty-eighth Street Theatre
    Located on Fifty-eighth street, and occupying nearly an entire block from Third street * to Lexington avenue. This theatre, favored by residential location, is one of the most popular amusement resorts north of Forty-second street. It is devoted to All-Star Vaudeville

---
* The word "street" is a misprint for "avenue."

and a well-known catch line to its patrons is "Here we see all they have at other houses, and 'more besides.'"

Proctor's One Hundred and Twenty-fifth Street Theatre

Located on the "Uptown" Broadway, this theatre is probably the most popular of the entire circuit. Its ideal stock organization, guided by expert direction, has become an astonishing success. The play here changes weekly and high class vaudeville is presented during the intermissions.

Proctor's Newark Theatre

This playhouse is recognized everywhere as having the most fashionable clientele of any vaudeville theatre in America. Favored with central location and a perfect auditorium, this playhouse holds a unique position on Mr. Proctor's famous circuit.

Proctor's Albany Theatre

It is with pardonable pride that Mr. Proctor points to this theatre, which has become a landmark in the State capital. This was his initial venture and from it sprang an historic career.

Proctor's Troy Theatre

This is the latest acquisition to Mr. Proctor's circuit and as his style of vaudeville entertainment is a distinct innovation to Troyeans, the little playhouse has met with splendid success.

Proctor's All-Star Players

This organization, permanently located at Proctor's Fifth Avenue Theatre, is considered the finest resident company ever seen. Its personnel includes many successful stars and every production made is characterized by careful preparation and intelligent study. It is Mr. Proctor's ambition to have this organization rank in future theatrical records with those of Augustin Daly, A. M. Palmer and Wallack's.

Proctor's Harlem Company

Permanently located at Mr. Proctor's up-town theatre, and priding itself in a unique popularity. Here the productions are usually a duplicate of those seen at the Fifth Avenue Theatre, and with the same careful preparation.

ANNOUNCEMENT

Proctor's Fifth Avenue Theatre

Mr. Proctor wishes to take advantage of this means of announcing the attractive offerings arranged at this theatre for the immediate future.

For Easter week, beginning Monday, April 16th, a gala double programme has been arranged for the *Proctor All-Star Players,* as follows:

Monday, Tuesday and Wednesday, matinees and evenings
"The Prisoner of Zenda"
Thursday, Friday and Saturday, matinees and evenings
"Rupert of Hentzau"
And every afternoon and evening during the Holiday week
Yvette Guilbert

Will appear during one of the intermissions.

Special—Commencing Monday matinee, April 23rd, Mr. Proctor announces the greatest production ever made by an American Stock Company, of
"Joan of Arc"

(End of Act 4)

ACT FIVE

Double Harness

Early in 1906, when the Fifth Avenue Theatre, Mr. Proctor's most important playhouse, was bought out from under him by his chief rival, B. F. Keith, the forces of Proctor and Keith were joined. Keith had formed a corporation under the name of International Amusement and Real Estate Company, and its acquisition of Proctor's Fifth Avenue Theatre brought about the partnership which Mr. Proctor had avoided until he had to make the choice between joining the opposition or losing his key theatre. Proctor had leased the famous playhouse in 1900 from the Gilsey Estate for a period of twelve years, but the estate reserved the right to terminate the lease on a year's notice of the sale of the property.

J. Austin Fynes, once associated with Mr. Proctor and now again employed by Keith, acted as a go-between for the formation of the Keith and Proctor Amusement Company. Up to this time, Mr. Proctor had picked his own partners in his own good time—George Mansfield, Henry R. Jacobs, Charles Frohman, David Belasco and others—all harmonious associations, serving the mutual aims of the partners and proving highly satisfactory to all concerned. This forced alliance with Keith was a different matter.

Proctor decided it might be wiser to join his rival than to try to continue his own independent way and oppose a newly-strengthened opponent, who had an impressive chain of theatres under his control and might subject him to an all-out war in bookings and in competition with Keith houses in all key locations.

PROCTOR'S 23d ST. THEATRE

PROCTOR'S 23d ST. THEATRE
23d Street, Near 6th Ave.
ABSOLUTELY FIREPROOF & SAFE.
PROCTOR & TURNER, - - - Proprietors and Managers.

The Great Metropolis

Messrs. Proctor & Turner take pleasure in announcing to their patrons that the Second Season of

PROCTOR'S NEW 23d ST. THEATRE

will be inaugurated on August 31st, with an elaborate production of Messrs. Jessop & Teal's Drama,

The Great Metropolis

a local play of New York of to-day, which will be presented under the personal managerial direction of Messrs. Klaw & Erlanger.

"The Great Metropolis" promises to be one of the most important dramatic productions of next season, and nothing will be spared to give it the benefit of all the accessories of an excellent cast, elaborate scenery, etc., etc.

PROCTOR'S 23RD ST. THEATRE.

MONDAY EVENING,

June 17th,

Dockstadter's * Minstrels.

Mr. Lou. Dockstadter

and Company.

40 ARTISTS.

PROCTOR'S 23rd STREET THEATRE

PROGRAMME.

PROCTOR & TURNER, - - - Proprietors and Managers.

Week Ending June 15th, 1889.
Matinees at 2 o'clock.   Every Evening at 8.15 o'clock.
Matinee: SATURDAY.

15th WEEK   OF THE ECCENTRIC COMEDIAN,   15th WEEK

NEIL BURGESS

AND A SPECIALLY SELECTED COMPANY.
— UNDER THE MANAGEMENT OF —
DAVID TOWERS,
— IN —

"THE COUNTY FAIR"

A Picture of New England Life by
CHARLES BARNARD.

CAST OF CHARACTERS:

Otis Tucker	Archie Boyd
Tim, the Tanner	Charles J. Jackson
Solon Hammerhead	James Mahoney
Joel Bartlett	Hal Clarendon
Bill Parker	A. F. Horn
Bub	Will McKay
Johnnie Perkins	Allie Phillipps
Constable	Britton Stevens
Jockey Joe	F. Lynch
Cold Molasses	By Himself
Tagg	Clara Thropp
Sally Greenaway	May Taylor
Maria Perkins	Addie Phillipps
Sarah Wilkins	Edith Wilson
Abigail Prue, (prim prudish and practical)	Neil Burgess

Programme Continued on Page 7.

A TRIPLE PROGRAM, 1889

379 6th Avenue, 3rd Door above 23rd Street.

Office and Sales Rooms, Cor. 1st Avenue & 74th Street.
Received Highest Honors at World's Fair.

PROCTOR'S THEATRE.
Special Announcement!!

The patrons of this theatre will enjoy the
Very Best Attractions
obtainable in America and Europe. The managements translation of the word Vaudeville is
Grand Opera, Variety,
Opera Bouffe, Acrobatic Acts,
Minstrelsy, Music, Comedy, etc.
Every branch of the amusement profession will be represented each week, and in whatever line
ONLY FIRST-CLASS ARTISTS
Will appear.
The Entertainments will always be of the highest and most refined order and particularly suited to
Ladies and Children.
The entertainments will be fully equal to those in other houses where the price of seats is $1.00 and $1.50. The management has recently secured a number of the
BEST and HIGHEST SALARIED ARTISTS IN ALL EUROPE
and they will soon appear. The Sunday Newspapers of New York and vicinity will regularly contain a full list of the various artists appearing in the entertainments each week.

LOOK OUT FOR PLEASANT SURPRISES.
PRICES—Balcony 25c., Orchestra 50c.,
Box Seats $1.00.
Come At Any Time
REMAIN AS LONG AS YOU PLEASE.
From 10 A. M. to 10:30 P. M. Daily.

F. F. PROCTOR, Proprietor and Manager.
JAMES F. TIGHE,—General Stage Director.

SOHMER PIANO USED HERE.

MASON & HAMLIN ORGAN USED HERE.

R. H. Macy & Co's advertisement in this programme may prove interesting to you

Received Highest Honors at World's Fair

PROCTOR'S THEATRE.
Fall and Winter Season
AN ENORMOUS SUCCESS
resulting from the introduction of

LIVING PICTURES
in the continuous Performances at this POPULAR FAMILY RESORT, has determined Mr. PROCTOR to retain them as

A PERMANENT FEATURE
New subjects being added in rapid succession.
They will be supplemented by

High - Class - Vaudeville
in the best and most comprehensive sense of the term, embracing

NOVELTIES OF ALL KINDS
Operettas, Variety, Acrobatic Acts, Minstrelsy, Music and Comedy, the BEST OBTAINABLE in Europe and America.
Every class of entertainers will be represented and

ONLY FIRST-CLASS ARTISTS
will be selected. Realizing that the permanent patronage of PROCTOR'S THEATRE is largely composed of

Ladies and Children,
who can always attend without escort, the aim of the management will be to offer only

Refined Entertainment
Kept scrupulously free from any gross or objectionable features.

Always Something Diverting
and of a standard of merit equal to, and often surpassing, the attractions offered at other houses for $1.00 and $1.50.

Complete Changes Every Week.
that will be fully announced in the Sunday Newspapers of New York and vicinity.

LOOK OUT FOR PLEASANT SURPRISES.
PRICES—Balcony 25c., Orchestra 50c., Box Seats $1.00.

ANOTHER POPULAR INNOVATION.

NEW BALCONY STALLS
Seating from four to six persons each, for the special benefit of family parties.

Come At Any Time
REMAIN AS LONG AS YOU PLEASE.
From 10 A. M. to 10:30 P. M. Daily.

SUNDAY SACRED CONCERTS
Every Sunday,
Continuous from 2 to 10.30 P. M.

Always Crowded.

F. F. PROCTOR, Proprietor and Manager.
JAMES F. TIGHE,—General Stage Director.

ALWAYS IN THE LEAD

LIVING PICTURES

PROCTOR'S

THE HOME OF PERPETUAL ENTERTAINMENT,

Presenting the Latest Novelties

In rapid succession has resumed
Its well defined and always popular policy of offering CONTINUOUS HIGH-CLASS VAUDEVILLE from 10 A. M. to 10.30 P. M.; Supplemented by Mr. PROCTOR'S

New Second Series

LIVING PICTURES

3 TIMES DAILY

DISCLOSED AT 12 NOON, 4 P. M. AND 10 P. M.

The Early Noon Exhibition is for the special accomodation of Ladies Visiting the Great Down-Town Shopping District during the Morning hours.

For the new subjects in THE HUMAN ART GALLERY Mr. Proctor has secured new models, new backings and new paraphernalia, including a magnificent colossal LOUIS XIVth, frame of gold and tufted velvet, displayed within a cabinet hung with 1800 yards of the most costly satin and silken plush.

The pictures are under the artistic supervision of MISS SUSIE KIRWIN.

ALL NEW PICTURES

In the $10,000 Series

And Many More to Follow.

Special Announcement!

Musical Living Pictures,

For example when "Coming Thro' the Rye," and "The Village Blacksmith" are shown, with living figures, the appropriate melodies will be sung by invisible soloists and quartettes.

The Latest Sensation in London.

LIVING PICTURES

PROCTOR'S ALL THE TIME

PROCTOR'S Ladies Club Theatre
23rd STREET, NEAR SIXTH AVE.

APPROPRIATE SACRED
Sunday ✱ Entertainments

Will be given in PROCTOR'S THEATRE

EVERY SUNDAY

The very best talent will contribute to the entertainments and there will be nothing objectionable to the most refined tastes.

The entertainments will be continuous. Come when you wish and stay as long as you please, just as you do to the Vaudeville Entertainments during the week.

Prices as usual 50c., 25c., 15c.

DO YOU WEAR KNOX HATS?

1894

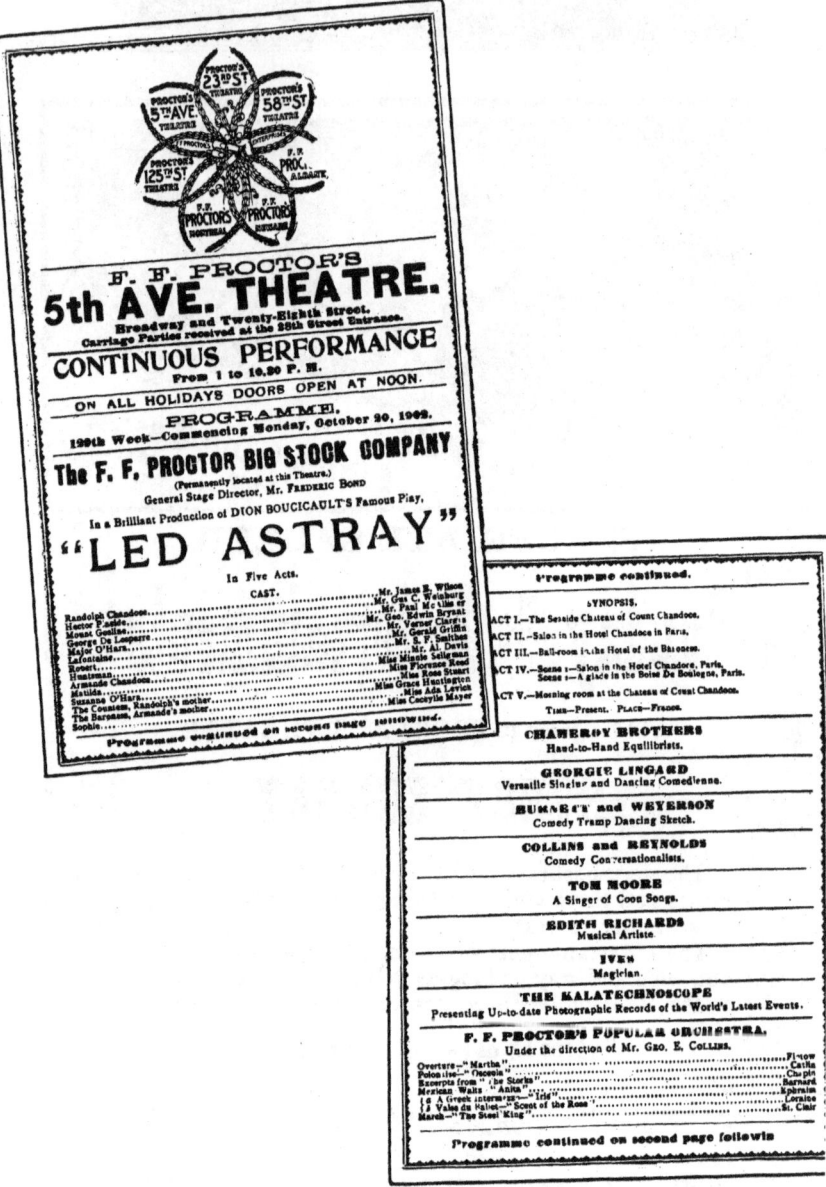

When Georgie Lingard Played Proctor's Fifth Avenue Theatre, 1902

A striking and unusual picture is that presented in this week's MIRROR, showing the façade of Proctor's Newark theatre as illuminated by countless electric lamps at night. Many photographic difficulties have been overcome in making this handsome picture, and an excellent idea is conveyed of the attractiveness of the theatre, which fronts upon Military Park, in the heart of the New Jersey city. The effect of the nightly illumination is one to make all passers pause and to draw thousands of them inside the house. Manager Proctor's Newark venture has proved successful beyond expectation, and from the opening performance the theatre has been filled almost always to capacity. At one of the first performances the crowd was so great that when the doors were opened the inrushing people wrecked the ticket office and the picture frames in the lobby and caused General Manager J. Austin Fynes to issue orders that doors should be opened a half-hour earlier than had been deemed necessary.

Proctor Plans Stage Innovation

JAN 28 1925

Is to Give Stock Production, a Film Play and Vaudeville for Single Admission.

Those who take in the show at Proctor's Twenty-third Street Theater after February 9 will see for the price of one admission a stock company production, a six reel super-screen and four acts of vaudeville.

This new program is to be inaugurated in the famous old variety house on West Twenty-third street, near Seventh avenue, by F. F. Proctor, veteran showman, director of the F. F. Proctor Theatrical Enterprises, including fourteen theaters in and around this city, and vice-president of the Keith-Albee Booking Agency.

An announcement of Mr. Proctor's experiment read in part:

"The policy about to be installed at this house is something entirely new and novel. The theatergoing public have been given stock companies for many years; they have been able to see vaudeville and pictures and theaters devoted exclusively to pictures, but never before have they been able to enter a theater and for the one price of admission witness all th[e] ... presented after ...

... as heretofore, through the Keith-Albee Agency and only the best will be engaged.

"Once be[fore] well known form of en[tertainment] some of th[e] present da[y] to a New[...] ward beca[me] stage and [...] We are s[...] and 1892, [...] Stock Co[mpany] Twenty-th[ird] time such [...] Ada Reha[n] more, W[...] Stevenson[...] Boucicaul[t] Frances Fairbank[s] ...

YORK COMMER[CIAL]

Mostly Personal.

Of all New York's busy business men few can justly lay claim to a more strenuous life than Frederick Freeman Proctor, the well-known theatrical manager and proprietor of seven theaters. His "every business morning" includes every morning in the year, and his busy days number three hundred and sixty-five in a twelve month.

Mr. Proctor is a showman, trained from early youth, and is a past master in every branch of the theatrical business. His seven theatres include the Fifth Avenue, the Twenty-third Street, the Fifty-eighth Street and the One Hundred and Twenty-fifth Street in this city, one in Albany, one in Newark, N. J., and one in Montreal.

Mr. Proctor was born in Dexter, Maine about fifty years ago. His father was a physician in that town, and one of its foremost citizens. Young Proctor migrated to Boston—that Mecca of all New England boys—when a very young man, and obtained employment in a large dry goods store. He made something of a mark, as a boy, in commercial life, but an evening spent at a per[formance]...

N. Y. Tribune July 11, 1912

$5,000 VAUDEVILLE OFFER

F. F. Proctor Puts Up Record S[u]m to Bring New Blood to Vaudev[ille].

A stir of interest was aroused ye[sterday] at the announcement by F. F. Procto[r], the vaudeville manager, of $5,000 for any sensational novelty feature worth that sum to appear at his Fifth Avenue Theatre during the week of August 12.

The offer is open to every artist or combination of artists, although Mr. Proctor would prefer an American or an American organization.

No restrictions are attached to Mr. Proctor's offer, the only condition being that the attraction must be worth $5,000. As $3,000 has hitherto been the top price for vaudeville, the somebody or bodies must be $2,000 better than Eva Tanguay, Bayes and Norworth, Albert Chevalier, Harry Lauder, Elsie Janis, Yvette Guilbert, Nat Goodwin, Fay Templeton or Lillian Russell to be worth the sum.

The offer is open to the Friars or Lambs' clubs to repeat their recent frivols. Grand opera artists are invited to submit propositions, and any one else who can honestly claim to be a $5,000 feature is invited to qua[lify ...] forma[nce ...] Hanlon b[rothers, acrobats] at one of the theaters, operated to change the current of his life. He was then about seventeen years old. He began a course of training at the Young Men's Christian Association gymnasium, and in the course of a year he had become proficient in all sorts of acrobatic work. With another youngster of his own age he perfected a "team" on the horizontal bars and the two young men got an engagement at a theater in Boston, under the name of the "Ju[ve]nantine Brothers." They ...

The magnitude of this merger and the contemporary view of the main figures in it may be gathered from the following paragraphs selected from a long news story in the May 13th, 1906, issue of the New York *Morning Telegraph.*

> The long expected has come to pass. Vaudeville's generals, B. F. Keith and F. F. Proctor, have joined hands in their New York City interests, and all the metropolitan houses formerly controlled by them, together with Mr. Keith's recently acquired Jersey City playhouse, the Bijou, will in future be marshalled under the widespread banner of "The Keith & Proctor Theatres."
>
> This initial movement toward what seems to be an ultimate merger of great Eastern, Central and Western properties, includes the affiliation of Keith's Union Square Theatre, Proctor's Fifth Avenue, Proctor's Twenty-third Street, Proctor's Fifty-eighth Street, Proctor's 125th Street and Mr. Keith's latest Eastern acquisition, the Bijou, in Jersey City. . . .
>
> There will be a new vaudeville playhouse in Broadway's very heart, and it will be a Keith & Proctor playhouse, so costly, so luxurious, so complete, so up-to-the-very-second that no other city in the world will be able to offer its equal. . . .
>
> Under the terms of yesterday's compact, which is to cover a term of ten years, with renewals amply provided for, Mr. Keith's Union Square playhouse, the four Proctor houses in this city and the recently purchased Keith Bijou Theatre in Jersey City are merged under the general name of "The Keith & Proctor Theatres," the titles to which are vested in a new corporation just formed under the Delaware laws. The stock in this corporation will be equally divided between Mr. Keith and Mr. Proctor. The assets of the company will be the leases, trademarks and goodwill of all the theatres named above, and they will at once be operated under one general direction.
>
> Mr. Keith does not include his Boston or Philadelphia houses in this alliance, nor does Mr. Proctor contribute his Newark, Albany or Troy theatres, except in the B. F. Keith booking office. It only happened that Jersey City was deemed a factor in the local "combine" because of its nearness to the great metropolis, and because also Mr.

Keith had so recently acquired it that it had hardly been enrolled under his banner.

The bookings of all the theatres in this new alliance, together with those of the remaining Proctor theatres, seven in all, will be made from today through the B. F. Keith booking office in the St. James Building. Mr. Keith thus increases to thirty-five his list of theatres to be supplied with a weekly change of vaudeville artists of the higher grade. It is fine for the artist.

In the formation of this new company, the financial strength of which reaches into many figures, arrangements of a minor nature have yet to be completed. It is officially announced, however, that the general manager of the new corporation, and hence of all the theatres newly allied, will be Edward F. Albee. He is already, and has been for many years, Mr. Keith's general manager. By the recent merger he thus becomes general manager of about twenty playhouses besides the B. F. Keith booking office. He will have lots to do, and everybody agrees that he will do it well. Naturally, he will surround himself with a strong staff of assistants, but he has not definitely announced the personnel of his staff. . . .

In the erection and completion of the new Keith & Proctor vaudeville palace in this city, Mr. Albee's ability will be particularly valuable. . . .

Let us see, meanwhile, what manner of men they are who have done this—their early environment, their training and the general circumstances under which they have arrived at what has now happened. Both are New England born—Benjamin Franklin Keith, in New Hampshire, and Frederick Freeman Proctor, in Maine; and both saw the first light of day less than sixty years ago. Their early lives ran in almost identical grooves, for both were bred on farms, both left home early; both became enamored of show life while still in their 'teens, and both found in the white tents of the circus the same fascination which made millionaires of Barnum, Bailey, Cole, Hutchinson, Forepaugh, the Ringlings and many others.

Mr. Keith's early experiences were full of vicissitudes; so were Mr. Proctor's. The former, however, laid his plans along managerial lines, from which he never afterward departed, while Mr. Proctor at first became a performer, the best in his line—they say who recall his work —that America or Europe ever saw.

Mr. Keith entered management on his own account in Boston in 1883; Mr. Proctor, forsaking the stage, perhaps a year or so earlier, had leased a little theatre in Albany. Mr. Keith exhibited to the Hub public at 10 cents a head a midget "Baby Alice" and thus started in a room 15 x 35 feet what is now his superb circuit of theatres.

Mr. Proctor, too, was successful in extracting many dimes from the close pockets of Albanians, and thus laid the foundation of his present splendid properties. The rest is pleasantly told theatrical history. In Boston Keith has had twenty-three years of unbroken success. The little 10-cent store of 1883 now has its apotheosis in a theatre involving a paid-up investment of nearly a million dollars—a theatre of which the late Sir Henry Irving wrote in the visitors' register: "This is the most magnificent playhouse in the world." In Albany the dimes of his early patrons long ago enabled Proctor to buy the handsomest theatre in town.

Both these men branched out early, Keith to Providence, then to Philadelphia, then to New York, later to Cleveland and between times even to London, where he astounded the lawyers of the Duke of Bedford by laying down in hard cash the entire purchase price of "the dear old Princess Theatre," the historic scene of Wilson Barrett's greatest triumphs. Such a transaction, so much ready money, was unheard of in London realty deals; but it was not a new business to Mr. Keith. And he has since been doing lots of bigger things, too, such as the building of another million-dollar playhouse in Philadelphia and the acquirement of houses in Cleveland, Columbus, Portland, Me., Jersey City, Manchester, N. H., and other places too numerous to mention.

Yet Mr. Proctor seems to have kept along well in this march of managerial progression. From the little Albany theatre he extended his operations quickly and wisely until he found himself the head center of a circuit of 10, 20 and 30-cent playhouses that became famous in their day, as well they might, for that circuit at one time embraced a full score of theatres all under the Proctor banner. In New York City he made his entry in 1888 at his Twenty-third street house. Today he owns outright two theatres and leases two more in the greatest theatrical metropolis in the world. . . .

* * *

Now, as part of a vastly expanded empire, Mr. Proctor gave more and more of his time to investigating the trends in public taste regarding things theatrical. In the late summer of 1907, he made a trip to New England; as reported in the New York *Morning Telegraph* of August 29th, it shows his apparent enthusiasm for the new United Booking Offices and his belief in the future of vaudeville.

F. F. Proctor and Mrs. Proctor, yesterday finished a twenty-five hundred mile autoing tour through New England. They left Larchmont a month ago in a 30-horsepower Rainier machine. . . . In the New England cities visited by Mr. Proctor, notably New Haven, Providence, Springfield, Worcester and Hartford, he reported an amazing briskness in vaudeville.

"It is altogether remarkable to observe the hold vaudeville has obtained in these provincial centers, where there are great industrial interests," said Mr. Proctor. "No doubt this fondness for vaudeville is due, in large part, to the exceedingly moderate-priced theatres on the Poli Circuit, for instance, Connecticut and Massachusetts, where an enormous clientele has been secured by always maintaining these small prices.

"In addition, the ability of the United Booking Offices to furnish attractions for these smaller towns equally as imposing as those demanded by the big houses in the great metropolitan centers, strengthens immeasurably the prestige of the provincial house.

"Every city of any commercial importance throughout New England has its own vaudeville theatre offering all the stars of the United Booking Offices in splendidly arranged programmes that vie with Broadway vaudeville in every respect save the price.

"I never felt surer of the outlook for vaudeville than now," said Mr. Proctor, "after a careful inspection of these hustling cities, where an air of general prosperity is distinctly observable in every channel of trade and commerce."

* * *

The United Booking Offices had virtual control of the vaudeville situation in the East for many years. Because Messrs. Proctor and Keith owned theatres, they were in a position to exact commissions for booking vaudeville acts that added greatly to their fortunes. But Mr. Proctor, though an official of this organization, always preserved the autonomy of his own theatres, and the Proctor circuit was never a part of the Keith circuit, making its booking arrangements with the Keith organization.

As the years rolled along, Mr. Proctor found himself less able to see eye to eye with Keith. The organizational setup of the Keith and Proctor Amusement Company (B. F. Keith, President; F. F. Proctor, Vice President; Paul Keith, Treasurer; F. F. Proctor, Jr., Secretary, and George E. Wallen, Assistant Treasurer) provided that the Executive Committee, Mr. Keith and Mr. Proctor, should run the theatres and that any points of dispute that could not be settled between them would be arbitrated.

In the winter of 1910–11, Mr. Proctor instructed Clarence Wallen to employ the most eminent counsel procurable and sue for dissolution of the partnership. The case dragged along for almost a year and a half and cost Mr. Proctor about $60,000 in fees. It was tried in Maine—at Portland and, on appeal, at Augusta—near Mr. Proctor's birthplace. The major incidents in the long litigation are described in the following press clipping excerpts.

(From the *New York World* of February 19, 1911)

(Special to The World)

Portland, Me., Feb. 18.—Leaders in the vaudeville theatre world with eminent counsel, including Judge Morgan J. O'Brien of New

York, appeared before Supreme Justice Peabody here today at a hearing on the disagreement between B. F. Keith and Frederick F. Proctor in their amusement combine. The hearing is on a petition to vacate the temporary receivership for the combine decreed Dec. 31.

Mr. Proctor has asked a dissolution of the combine, alleging fraud and mismanagement on the part of Mr. Keith. The latter enters a general denial.

As Mr. Keith is in Florida an affidavit was read from him. Those who offered affidavits partial to Mr. Keith's side were Walter J. Donovan, General Manager of the Keith circuit; Ethan M. Robinson, former manager for Proctor; John N. Clancy, U. Grant Blackford, Abraham L. Erlanger, Edward F. Albee and Lee Shubert.

The Proctor side of the case was outlined at the afternoon session. It was alleged that Mr. Keith is the chief owner in the International Amusement and Realty Company of New York, which bought the Fifth Avenue Theatre building and then refused the combine a renewal of the lease. It was denied that the Proctor houses were in poor condition at the time of the combine. One argument offered was that the Proctor idea was to spend money on the acts, while Keith made a play for beautiful interiors to his theatres.

Affidavits concerning Proctor as a theatrical manager were read from no less well known authorities than Daniel Frohman, William Morris, Henry B. Harris, Joseph M. Weber, Lee Shubert, William Harris and Joseph Bird. The hearing will be continued Monday.

* * *

(From the *New York Sun*, July 28, 1911)

Portland, Me., July 27.—The litigation between B. F. Keith and F. F. Proctor before the Maine Supreme Court was brought to a settlement today by agreement of counsel and the sanction of the court.

The Keith & Proctor Amusement Company will be dissolved and Keith and Proctor will receive back the theatres controlled and owned by them at the time of the formation of the company and contributed by them to its assets.

A five year lease of the Harlem Opera House acquired by the company after its organization was disposed of by sealed bids, with only Keith and Proctor allowed to bid. Keith's bid of $41,000 was the higher.

Under the arrangement referred to Keith will get the Union Square and Jersey City theatres and Proctor the 125th street, the Fifty-eighth street and the Twenty-third street theatre.

The only matter unsettled is control of the Fifth Avenue Theatre. This will be decided by Justice Bird, and pending his decision it will be managed by the incumbent, Edward F. Albee.

* * *

(From the *New York Tribune*, July 29, 1911)

Final arguments of the attorneys in the Keith & Proctor Amusement Company dissolution suit on the question of the disposition of the Fifth Avenue Theatre property will be heard before the Supreme Court of Maine, in Portland, beginning Augsut 10. B. F. Keith and F. F. Proctor will again go their separate ways, the former assuming ownership in two New York houses, the Union Square Theatre and the Harlem Opera House, and the latter holding the Twenty-third street theatre, the Fifty-eighth street and the East One Hundred and Twenty-fifth street theatres.

Mr. Proctor was elated yesterday over what he regarded as a big victory in the courts, and he was already busy on plans for the refurnishing of his house and several innovations.

"Until the final settlement in regard to the Fifth avenue house is made," he said, "it, of course, will remain under the direct management of Edward F. Albee, under the supervision of myself and Mr. Keith. My other theatres, however, will be at once put in the best possible shape. The policy of providing the highest class of entertainment, which I have always advocated and practised, will be continued. There will be no change in my prices."

Mr. Proctor now has twenty amusement enterprises and is interested in one hundred more.

* * *

F. F. PROCTOR

(From the New York Morning Telegraph, October 20, 1911)
(Special Dispatch to The Morning Telegraph)

Portland, Me., Oct. 19.

Justice George S. Bird, of the Maine Supreme Court, today handed down a decision in the Proctor-Keith suit over the lease of the Fifth Avenue Theatre in New York City, awarding the property to F. F. Proctor for the balance of the term of five years.

The story of the disagreements which led to the dissolution of the partnership formed in June, 1906, to continue ten years, between F. F. Proctor and B. F. Keith, magnates in the vaudeville world, is the history of one of the bitterest managerial controversies of recent years.

It was brought out during the progress of the case that shortly before the conclusion of the partnership arrangements, Mr. Keith formed the International Amusement and Realty Company, and purchased the Fifth Avenue Theatre Building from the Gilsey estate, from which Mr. Proctor held his lease, for $1,300,000.

Mr. Proctor turned over this lease to the Keith & Proctor Company, later obtaining a new five-year lease.

Attorneys for Mr. Keith contended that the property was not an original contribution of Mr. Proctor's to the firm, and should be put at auction under the partnership agreement.

After the news of the decision reached this city, F. F. Proctor, Jr., said:

"We are just as confident of the confirmation of the ruling of Judge Bird, as we have always been, that the lease would be awarded to us. Should this be the ultimate result the theatre will be run under F. F. Proctor's personal direction as a high-class vaudeville theatre."

E. F. Albee said for Mr. Keith, of whose interests he is the general manager:

"For the present I continue the manager, representing both Messrs. Keith and Proctor. We expect a reversal in the higher court, but in the event of Mr. Proctor's ultimate victory there the theatre reverts in 1916 to Mr. Keith, the owner of the property."

* * *

DOUBLE HARNESS

(From the *New York Herald*, May 11, 1912)

Maine's Court of Appeals, sitting in Augusta, yesterday dismissed Mr. B. F. Keith's appeal from its decision awarding to his one time business associate, Mr. F. F. Proctor, possession of the Fifth Avenue Theatre under a five year lease.

When Messrs. Keith and Proctor came to the parting of the ways, more than a year ago, and their properties were ordered redistributed, there was a contest as to which should receive the Fifth Avenue, the lease of which was held by Mr. Proctor, with option of renewal. The owner was and is the International Amusement Company, which is really Mr. Keith, who also owns half of the Broadway block in which the Fifth Avenue stands. The Maine courts, in which the litigation originated, awarded the theatre to Mr. Proctor. Mr. Keith appealed and that appeal now has been dismissed. So Mr. Proctor gets the Fifth Avenue Theatre for something more than four years more, when possession goes back to Mr. Keith. Mr. Proctor also is to receive the profits of the theatre since Mr. Keith's appeal last November.

Mr. W. F. S. Hart, principal counsel for Mr. Proctor, said last night: "The decision of the highest court in Maine gives to Mr. Proctor every point claimed by him from the start of this litigation, eighteen months ago. It also carries with it the very valuable territorial franchise covered by agreements between the managers comprised in the United Booking Offices. In other words, Mr. Proctor is protected against outside vaudeville invasion in the section south of Forty-second street as far as Union Square, and he is, of course, at liberty to build on his own account in that section should he feel so inclined."

Since the litigation started Mr. Keith and associates have purchased the eight theatres in New York and Brooklyn owned by Mr. Percy G. Williams and greatly strengthened his position in the vaudeville field. At the same time both men are members of the United Booking Offices, the corporation that supplies them with attractions. Asked as to Mr. Proctor's status in the latter corporation under the new conditions, Mr. Hart said:

"Mr. Proctor stands as he always did—on his own ground. He has an unassailable voting power in the big booking office, which no combination or coalition—friendly or otherwise—can in any way affect during the life of the corporation that operates the United Booking Offices. The recent Williams-Keith deal, therefore, has no direct bearing upon Mr. Proctor's arrangements or properties."

Mr. Proctor announced yesterday that improvements will immediately be begun at the Fifth Avenue. The theatre will be renovated, the aim being to make it one of the most attractive in New York. In addition to this theatre Mr. Proctor controls three other vaudeville houses in New York—the Twenty-third Street Theatre, the Fifty-eighth Street Theatre and the One Hundred and Twenty-fifth Street Theatre.

It also is announced that Mr. Proctor has acquired a site in Mount Vernon upon which he intends erecting a vaudeville theatre to cost $300,000. This, with others of his theatres in Albany, Schenectady and Newark, will form an important chain of playhouses.

An improvement is planned for the Fifty-eighth Street Theatre, as Italian gardens are to be added to the roof.

* * *

Mr. Proctor now branched out with additional theatres in suburban towns—Mt. Vernon, Yonkers, Newark, Plainfield and Elizabeth—always on the policy of continuous vaudeville at cheap prices.

Robert Grau, in his book *The Business Man in the Amusement World* (Broadway Publishing Company, 1910) tells of Mr. Proctor's success with suburban theatres. In Mount Vernon, New York, which had been Mr. Grau's home, no theatre had made a living until Mr. Proctor took over a house and introduced his "Bijou Dream" policy. After that a second theatre opened in Mount Vernon and did well. In short, Mr. Proctor's business ability actually benefited his competitors. Mount Vernon is cited by Mr. Grau as one of many smaller towns where Mr. Proctor—and then others—made profitable investments in variety theatres.

Again the constructive little reports began to appear in the newspapers. Here is one from the *New York Times* of August 5, 1911:

From the office of F. F. Proctor it was announced yesterday that work on a new theatre, at Bijou Park, Newark, will be begun in a short time. The estimated cost of the house is $1,000,000. This will make the twentieth amusement enterprise owned and controlled by Mr. Proctor who has an interest, it is said, in more than a hundred others.

* * *

As before, Mr. Proctor realized the prime necessity of keeping his playhouses well supplied with the best available talent and of finding, encouraging and developing the new talent. In the winter of 1912, a *New York Times* correspondent in London reported Mr. Proctor's plans as follows:

(BY MARCONI TRANSATLANTIC WIRELESS TELEGRAPH TO
THE NEW YORK TIMES)

LONDON, Feb. 4.—F. F. Proctor, head of the Proctor Vaudeville Circuit, is spending a few days in London looking over the vaudeville situation before going to Paris. Naturally he is taking in the theatres, music halls and other entertainments, but so far the prospects of obtaining fresh novelties, he said, were poor.

"While there has been a speedy growth in the tone of vaudeville, it is getting correspondingly difficult to obtain high class attractions. We don't know where to look for them. It seems the only field practically untouched is opera, so we will get hold of some great operatic singers."

Asked how New York music halls compared with those of London, Mr. Proctor replied:

"Very favorably. They are fully as high class as in London, with one distinct advantage. Admission prices are very much cheaper in New York than here, where the best halls get regular theatre prices. This is rather extraordinary, remembering that artists cost at least fifty per cent more in New York, while rents, orchestras, etc., are correspondingly higher."

Mr. Proctor thinks that London music halls have the advantage in being able to supply patrons with refreshments during the performance, which, as he puts it, "helps to keep the audience in good humor."

He thinks this innovation certain to be adopted in New York, though it may take some time yet; also smoking in all parts of the house instead of in the balconies only, as at present.

* * *

For the fall season of 1912 he made a remarkable deal with the London Palace in behalf of his Fifth Avenue Theatre. This is the story as run in the *New York Times* of September 9, 1912.

Through an arrangement with William Morris and Alfred Butt of London, F. F. Proctor has completed a deal for an interchange of vaudeville acts between the London Palace and the Fifth Avenue Theatre, New York.

Under the terms of the contracts the English acts are not to be seen at any other New York theatre until six months after their appearance at the Fifth Avenue. The first artist to come under this arrangement is Annette Kellerman in "Undine," which she has been giving at the Palace, London.

Miss Kellerman sailed for New York on the *Cedric* and will appear at the Fifth Avenue on Sept. 23. After a short tour of America she will go back to London for the Christmas pantomimes.

* * *

At home, too, Mr. Proctor was looking for striking and novel entertainments. In the summer of 1912 he made an astonishing offer which metropolitan newspapers actually ran as news on July 11th.

In the best of faith, F. F. Proctor comes forward with an offer of $5,000 a week for a really sensational vaudeville act. The offer, which at first seems to bear the mark of the press agent, developed upon investigation to be bona fide.

Mr. Proctor, it appears, has grown weary of the old acts and impatient at the apparent dearth of new features. He thinks that vaudeville should receive a stimulant, and he knows of no surer way to find one than to offer a huge sum of money for it.

He desires the new sensation for his bill at the Fifth Avenue Theatre during the week of August 12th.

The position is open to every player, producer or combination of players and producers in the world, although Mr. Proctor says he would prefer to pay the sum to an American.

Hitherto $3,000 has been considered the top salary for a vaudeville "act." Among those who have received that sum, or approximately that sum, for a week's salary are Eva Tanguay, Nora Bayes and Jack Norworth, Albert Chevalier, Harry Lauder, Yvette Guilbert, Lillian Russell and Nat Goodwin.

Mr. Proctor says that the Friars or the Lambs may receive the salary if they wish to repeat the important part of their recent entertainments, and also that he would like to hear from Grand Opera artists.

* * *

At the end of the same year Mr. Proctor's "help wanted" appeals took the form of the following article in the *New York Evening Journal* of December 24, 1912, with his portrait and his signature.

First-class or "big-time" vaudeville needs new blood, new faces, new ideas and new acts, and needs them all now. The manager of today is confronted with the proposition of creating new acts at new figures or going broke on the old ones at higher figures. One hears on all sides of the hight cost of living, but it is nothing as compared to the high cost of "old favorites" in vaudeville.

The headline act is booked on the strength of what it draws, and no act is too expensive if it brings in the money. It's the cost of the mediocre acts that hurts the managerial pocketbook, the one that costs $300 one season and tries to jump to $400 the next without a change of material in any part of the offering. These are the acts that fill the ranks of the agitators demanding their rights and wrangling over trifles without ever thinking of giving the public something new.

The public demands headliners, and headliners they must have—it is easy to create a headliner, but it's up to the headliner to maintain that proud position. The Fifth Avenue Theatre has the distinction of having created more headliners during the past season than any combination of theatres in the world, and right royally has the public responded.

The tremendous appeal of vaudeville is no myth, but the desires of vaudeville's followers must not be trifled with. In the absence of "sure-fire" headliners, the manager sometimes resorts to a bill of "old favorites," and sometimes the acts of the "old favorites" are so worn that it seems not only a pity to present them but a crime for the acts to take any money at the end of the engagement.

Small time is really the refuge for such offerings, but small time is now receiving more than its returns, taking ten old acts to sending back one good new act.

The biggest thing today in vaudeville is David Belasco's "The Drums of Oude," and where is the attraction to follow that sterling offering? The theatres are ready, the public is ready, but where is the producer with boldness and daring enough to hazard a new sensation? Mr. Belasco staked his artistic reputation on "The Drums of Oude," and won with highest honors and sure rewards. If Belasco, why not Frohman, Klaw and Erlanger, Savage, Brady, Shubert, Gaites or Dillingham? So far for the managers.

The biggest actors of today are either in vaudeville, have been in it, or are contemplating it, but the standard dramatists are somewhat shy in coming forward. There is big money awaiting Thomas, Broadhurst, Walter, Cohan, Rosenfeld, Sheldon, Forbes, Gillette, while there is no reason why Victor Herbert, Reginald de Koven, Luders or others of their calibre should not be furnishing musical attractions.

It is high time for something new in vaudeville, and the Fifth Avenue Theatre announces itself as the home of any meritorious novelty now in process of formation.

Vaudeville is absolutely the highest paid profession in the civilized world; it is the most liberally patronized of any branch of the amusement business, and it must continue to give twice the value received if it is to continue its glorious career.

* * *

In the year 1912 moving pictures were assuming some importance. Mr. Proctor had made many experiments with the new medium in its earliest days. He recognized the cinema's potential power, but he had great confidence in the future of vaudeville, as may be seen in an interview published in the *New York Morning Telegraph* of June 9, 1912. Note particularly the editorial emphasis on the keen business sense of Mr. Proctor, his independence, and, at the same time, his loyalty to United Booking.

At no time in the history of American theatricals has the vaudeville business assumed the interest and vast importance that it now holds. As a faithful recorder of the wonderful growth of this great amusement factor, *The Morning Telegraph* has made it clear that never before has the business of vaudeville reached the systematized perfection that it enjoys today.

In the group of brainy, far-seeing and quick-acting men who have brought about this condition, one of the most conspicuous in many respects is Frederick F. Proctor. A day or two ago a *Morning Telegraph* representative asked Mr. Proctor for an off-hand statement of his views of the general vaudeville situation, and the thoroughly informal chat that followed was decidedly interesting, because it began with a prediction on Mr. Proctor's part.

Mr. Proctor is neither an ambiguous, a loquacious nor a frequent talker for publication. In this characteristic, perhaps, he differs essentially from some of his theatrical confreres. When, therefore, one so usually reserved and diplomatically discreet ventures a prediction, it is worth while recording the fact.

"I take it for granted," said Mr. Proctor, "that nobody will deny that the most striking change in American theatricals during the past twenty-five years has been in the marvelous business development and artistic growth of what we call vaudeville. We simply can't argue about this. Our eyes and ears convince us, turn them wherever we may. The American public of many millions have settled any possible discussion. We don't even need statistics to prove it. Vaudeville is the one regnant form of the American theatrical entertainment."

"And your prediction—"

"Is that vaudeville's reign is in its infancy; that it will eventually and perpetually dominate all other forms of amusement, not only in the number of people it delights but also in the number it helps and profits. It is, I sometime think, like an auriferous mine whose surface has been barely scratched."

"You mean, then, that vaudeville is king?"

"Yes," said Mr. Proctor, "and has been for nigh on to a quarter of a century—almost without our realizing it."

There is a peculiar, quiet energy in Mr. Proctor's statements that is convincing. One reflects upon his long and varied theatrical career, and the conclusion is immediate that he speaks with absolute authority. He "knows the game"—perhaps a homely statement, but a concise one. For his knowledge of it is that of a lifetime, and he is yet in his prime; his study of it is as careful and keen now when he is a millionaire as it was thirty-six years ago when the dollar of today was hoarded for the rent of tomorrow.

In the compass of this man's vast and varied experience he has probably observed more changes in the public amusement taste than any other of his shrewd associates in the big vaudeville world of today. As performer and as manager, from a lowly start he has progressed with a sure and steady force that has made him the power he now is.

Among his fellow impresarios Proctor would seem to occupy a position at once unique and impressive. He was the pioneer of the lowest prices ever charged for wholesome theatricals; yet, as Charles Frohman's associate in the latter's earliest productions, he has seen the *haut ton* of Gotham's playgoers packing a Proctor playhouse to witness a Sardou premiere at grand opera prices.

How odd the march of years must seem to this man, who can still put his finger unerringly on the feverish pulse of the public and say:

"Vaudeville is King."

And he adds: "I have never been more certain of that fact than during the past few years. The enormous growth in the number of vaudeville theatres everywhere—large and small—has been a natural, healthy growth. The improvement in the quality of the entertainments has been a splendid one. These two facts fit together perfectly. The public spends its money more freely than ever. Theatre sites, rentals, artists' salaries, taxes and fixed charges generally are higher, but the gross receipts, after all, are about in keeping."

"And the net results?" was suggested.

"Are satisfactory to all concerned, whether performer, proprietor or public."

Which would seem to be a very frank and businesslike way of stating an absolute condition.

Indeed, there is always a thoroughly commercial, matter-of-fact manner in Mr. Proctor's discussion of theatricals. He would unquestionably protest at the conventional appellation of "Vaudeville Magnate," but it is nevertheless certain that he somehow suggests the merchant prince in his incisive speech, his quick facility in financial details, and his careful foresight as to business conditions.

Perhaps this is the natural result of his point of view. He says plainly that the olden type of "manager" has disappeared.

"We deal in amusements these days," he added, "as our great merchants deal in their wares. We must study the markets of the world, so that we may supply our customers—the public—with just what they want, and just when they want it. If they tire of a pattern we must change it to suit their capricious taste. And, like the great merchants, we, too, must buy our goods through the wholesaler. In our case it is that splendid clearing house, the United Booking Office."

It is a rather novel simile that Mr. Proctor uses, but a second thought justifies it. No doubt the gross daily receipts of a big vaudeville circuit like Proctor's, comprising about twenty-five prosperous houses, would compare quite favorably with the receipts of more than one of the city's great department stores.

Mr. Proctor's personal ownership or control of nearly all of his imposing chain of playhouses makes him by all means one of the most remarkable figures in the coterie of wealthy men who dominate the vaudeville business of the western hemisphere. For Proctor has no partners. He is not even fashionably incorporated—per se, or per anybody else. Standing sturdily alone in that respect he somehow calls to mind that canny Scot, Stevenson, the steel king, who alone lives to laughingly enjoy the distinction of having refused a partnership with Carnegie.

"I like a free rein," said Mr. Proctor, in a smiling reference to this fact. "Perhaps I work better in single harness. But by that I don't at all mean that I undervalue co-operation, or 'team work,' such as the leading vaudeville owners of America are now doing through the United Booking Office. That institution is, in my judgment, one of the most valuable of all factors in preserving the integrity and business system, as well as the harmony, of the vaudeville world.

"I am a staunch believer in its fundamental purpose, and I am glad to be able to say that we are faithfully and honestly working for the best interests of all concerned, among whom I include the thousands of artists whom it employs and protects."

Mr. Proctor is emphatic and earnest in his belief that the present peaceful condition of vaudeville affairs will continue for a very long period. There are no causes at issue, he said, and no reason why any shall arise.

As vice-president and a director of the United Booking Office, with a voting right that makes his personal power quite unassailable, he is nevertheless a constant advocate of the closest and most friendly relations between theatrical employers and performers. He does not overstate the strength of the big booking office. Its members are closely bound by twenty-year contracts, which still have sixteen years to run. And to this "clearing house," as he aptly phrases it, they must go as merchants to the wholesale market, there to select the best goods at the best prices, and there to enjoy the benefit of the protection which is accorded to both owners and artists.

Nobody can discuss this subject with him without at once discovering that Mr. Proctor's former stage experience has made him a fixed and loyal friend of the stage worker.

"Yes," he admitted when this was suggested, "it is doubtless true that I lean somewhat in that direction. I have every reason to do so.

DOUBLE HARNESS 115

In my long association with the men and women of the stage I have been very fortunate in their true friendship at all times. I often measure their hopes and ambitions with my own when I was one of them; and I am truly glad that as the years go by I am in a position to treat them as I would wish to have been treated long ago. Vaudeville has changed, indeed, but it can never change the real human nature that is the best element in the make-up of its people."

It is not surprising, then, to find in F. F. Proctor a very "safe and sane" optimist when vaudeville is discussed. His own plans, larger now than ever before, point to the constant extension of his enterprises; and his vigorous intellect and sturdy physique promise the full achievement of his purpose. In the petty politics and frothy gossip of the business he is never conspicuous. That is certainly characteristic of the successful merchant of the times.

* * *

Three years later the old question of Sunday closing came up again, this time in connection with the showing of moving pictures. The *New York World* of May 17, 1915, carried this paragraph about a Sunday closing law in a town where Mr. Proctor had a "Bijou Dream" house.

There were no moving pictures yesterday in Mount Vernon. F. F. Proctor, who had threatened to open his vaudeville house, kept his doors closed, because Supreme Court Justice Tompkins had upheld Mayor Fiske in his contention that he had a right to revoke the license of any theatre where Sunday motion pictures were shown. The fight will be carried to the Appellate Division.

* * *

In 1915 few theatres were devoting themselves to continuous vaudeville. Most houses had adopted the vaudeville and pictures policy and some were already devoted exclusively to the cinema. Mr. Proctor's able showmanship was speedily adapted to well-balanced programs including films—a modification of the variety idea. His success and originality in this field were well described by Mr. Grau in the *New York Morning Telegraph* of October 24th, 1915.

There is no question but that the present astonishing development in the exhibition of motion pictures is due greatly to that much abused term called "showmanship." Time was when the showman, speaking of him as an entity, was not reluctant to enter the field which has enriched so many inexperienced exhibitors. It is only within the last three years that the exploitation of the cameraman's productivity has been conducted with any discernment. More than one theatrical manager has "come a cropper" when utilizing theatrical methods for highgrade film offerings which should have been presented in a wholly different manner from the average release.

One of the first theatrical managers to use much discernment in the exhibition of picture plays was Frederick F. Proctor, who now conducts a chain of playhouses—twenty-five in number—most of which are within a few miles of New York, and in all of which the photoplay is featured.

As far back as 1906 Mr. Proctor was impressed with the importance of the new art, which at that time was still in the primitive stage; in fact it had just been discovered that stories of fiction and fact could be visualized in sequence on the screen. In that year, the Proctor house in West Twenty-third street began to rely almost entirely on film releases of the best available grade.

One hears little of the Proctor achievements in the field which has revolutionized the theatre because the Proctor management has not been partial to publicity, save in a distinctly local way. The writer is impressed with the object lesson to the modern exhibitor which a recital of the Proctor photo-play record would reveal. Twenty-five theatres, half of them resulting from success in motion picture exhibition, and six at least costing in no instance less than half a million dollars, have risen in the last three years, while three more amusement palaces, each seating in excess of 2,500 persons, are to be dedicated in November of this year.

On the theatrical Rialto F. F. Proctor is regarded as a shrewd showman, because with his ear to the ground he has always been able to fathom the trend. Although he has managed theatres for more than four decades he has never had a failure.

DOUBLE HARNESS 117

In film circles F. F. Proctor is hardly known at all. Never is he in evidence where and when the great problems of the film industry are being discussed; never has Mr. Proctor affiliated with others to strengthen his position. Not one of the manufacturers of film has ever had the right to claim a Proctor franchise. If he has ever met one of the barons of filmdom he cannot recall it.

Whence then comes the Proctor success? By what reckoning or system has this vaudeville magnate become a veritable pillar of the motion picture industry?

Showmanship in the selection of his attractions on stage or screen is the answer. When the Proctor patrons see a picture show they know that the programme will be scientifically blended, just as a Proctor vaudeville programme is. Never will the incongruity of two dramatic sketches conflicting with each other be on view in the Proctor vaudeville. It is precisely the same with a programme exclusively made up of picture plays. Always there is a perfect balance of comedy and serious films.

When one of the Proctor staff sees a particularly good feature film at a private showing he secures it no matter who is the maker of it. Even then it does not follow that this feature will be shown in every Proctor house, and surely not just because it has been contracted for.

That the Proctor photo-play programme is unique and constructive in its results, financially as well as artistically, is evidenced by the fact that a fair portion of the Proctor theatres do not now present any vaudeville at all, and each year the number of houses to abandon vaudeville is increased. Yet it is the vaudeville methods applied to Proctor's photo-play which have made the public response what it is.

It was the same Mr. Proctor who first began to use large and commodious playhouses in the smaller cities without having a single performer in the flesh. This is true of his "Bijou Dream" theatres, where photo-plays carefully selected provided the entire entertainment. It was the success in one of these Bijou Dreams that provided the incentive for the erection of the first million dollar amusement palace. This was in Mount Vernon, N. Y., and it is a concrete illustration of the trend in Proctor houses, when it is stated that this Labor Day is the first since the new house was erected that not a single vaudeville act is utilized, nor is there any announcement ahead of vaudeville for the future there. Moreover the number of Proctor houses entirely devoted to photo-plays is not only the largest it has ever been, but the newest and most costly of all the Proctor theatres are prospering on a plan of presenting feature photo-plays in the vaudeville way.

* * *

The "decline of vaudeville" is often dated from about 1915, and it is even more often interpreted as a result of the vogue of a more popular type of entertainment—the pictures. Anybody who studies Mr. Proctor's theory and practice in the theatre is likely to question these superficial explanations. He was at this time—as we have just seen in Mr. Grau's article—quite successfully applying his variety technique of well-balanced programs to the Bijou Dream houses in which he had introduced movies. His motto was still "Vaudeville is King"—or maybe more accurately "Variety is King"—and he was adding pictures in the manner of his variety programs of the earlier days so that the Proctor type of program (never static nor so set that it did not change with the times and popular tastes) was still profitable and supreme.

There is some truth in the notion that the very success of the Bijou Dream policy killed vaudeville, for this success came at a time when Mr. Proctor and other Variety princes were ready to retire, and the earnings in these houses coupled with the glamour of the cinema attracted Wall Street money into the variety business. Wall Street, once in control, dropped the managers who knew Proctor methods and put in their place men with no entertainment-business experience.

Besides, the moving-picture interests soon established a tight control of booking so that a theatre manager who attempted to make an independent and intelligent selection of films was bound to lose his franchise. Mr. Proctor had always preserved his independence of any attempt to monopolize or dictate about bookings.

If anybody could have saved Variety and Vaudeville, it was PROCTOR.

(End of Act 5)

ACT SIX

A Sterling Helpmate

At a time when Fred F. Proctor was already a professional performer with strong muscles, splendid physique, boyish charm of presentation and practical common sense, in Manhattan, a wholesome little girl with a pretty face was taking the first steps toward a career that was to parallel and then run concurrently with his.

On a rather warm night when most people in the old Bowery were sitting in the beer gardens or strolling along the pleasant street, this little girl, named Georgena Mills, but called Georgie by the kids, was turning cartwheels and back-somersaults to the applause of her playmates. Already she enjoyed the thrill of audience reaction. The bands in the beer gardens were playing nearby, and above the hand-clapping and singing of her playmates came their music to stir her to more eager rhythmic effort.

"Come on, Georgie, they're playing 'The Girl I Left Behind Me'," shouted one of her little friends.

"Let's see you skip," called another and put in Georgie's hand a piece of old clothesline. Then Georgie showed them skipping such as they had never seen before. The rope flashed over her head until it seemed a fine wisp of silvery moonlight. Her agile legs leaped into intricate dance patterns.

As the band started in with "Kingdom Coming," Georgie changed her routine. The blood of a trouper was already surging through her veins. Her rope-skipping and her fancy and acrobatic dancing were to take her into big-time circus and vaudeville, high romance, love, marriage, world travel with the King of Big Time Vaudeville, F. F. Proctor.

Georgie's uncle, James W. Lingard, was owner of the Bowery Theatre.* That fact apparently never helped her theatrical career, but the name Lingard was well known in the theatrical world, and she took it for stage purposes.

That "specialty act" for a motley crowd of neighborhood kids was her start—something like Fred Proctor's act on Boston Common. In 1873 when Georgie was twelve, she danced in the children's ballet of "Midsummer Night's Dream," in the Grand Opera House, at the corner of 8th Avenue and 23rd Street.

As she stepped out on the set, she probably knew that in the best seats in the house were sitting Jim Fiske himself, Jay Gould and the glamorous Josie Mansfield. No one had to tell her to put her best foot forward. She was thrilled with the spectacle all about her, with Fay Templeton running by lightly as Puck, and George Vivien, the stage manager, clapping his hands at them.

But Georgie's father was not pleased. He firmly believed that all theatrical people were headed for perdition. She was on the stage for a year at this time, playing with Jennie Hughes in "The French Spy," in "Little Lord Fauntleroy," and other plays. Then her father decided she must go back to school.

But even in school she had an opportunity to act. In patriotic school plays, coached by James Vincent, a very notable stage manager, she cut a neat figure in military uniform going through drills. At about the same time, Georgie got acquainted with a girl in her neighborhood who sang at concerts. With this girl's mother she went to several concerts. One day the mother asked Georgie: "Why don't you and Alice sing together? Maybe

---

* He played his "great original part" of Uncle Tom in October, 1866 at the New Bowery. That theatre burned in December of that year, and he died in 1870. There were other actors of the same family name, notably William Horace, the impersonator, and, in his troupe, Alice Dunning Lingard and Dickie Lingard, the former his wife and the latter her sister. Dickie later married Davison Dalziel, British M.P., head of the Dalziel News Agency. Nellie Lingard, Georgie's cousin, understudied Minnie Maddern Fiske as Tess.

A STERLING HELPMATE

I can get you a salary." For a while the two girls sang at various entertainments, and at this early age Georgie discovered that she could sing acceptably.

At sixteen she left school to learn dressmaking with the distinguished Madam Lane, who had an establishment at 29th Street off Broadway. Georgie got one dollar a week.

Georgie had to pick up the threads and pick out the bastings. After the girls went home she had to pick up the pins and make deliveries. (That reminds you of Fred Proctor's errand-boy evenings.) Madam Lane made dresses for wealthy women that commanded high prices, but she paid Georgie only a dollar a week, even after she had become a fitter. Madam Lane sometimes sent her to a customer's house for a fitting, but usually the customers came to her establishment in their open horse-drawn carriages. They were "very nice and gracious—more so than today," she says, and sometimes they gave her five or ten cents. After two years Georgie left Madam Lane, having won the friendship of "a particularly pleasant customer" who had taken a liking to her and who, years afterward went to Philadelphia and married a Mr. Hughes, who owned a theatre there. Mrs. Hughes kept in touch with Georgie, who had returned to theatrical work, and when show business carried Georgie to Philadelphia, Mrs. Hughes appealed to her husband, and he gave Georgie a week's engagement. It was then that she discovered that, beside her rope-skipping, her singing and dancing pleased her audiences.

Her next engagements were in German beer gardens and variety halls along the Bowery. The Volksgarten at 199–201 Bowery, where she sang in July of 1879, featured one or two singers, and once in a while a little play. The Bowery of that time was a respectable center of entertainment with a certain leisurely enjoyment of life and a charm that belongs to that time and can never be entirely recaptured.

Georgie urged a girl friend to introduce her to Michael Herrman, who ran the National Theatre, between Broome and Delancey Streets, across from the Pacific Garden.

Georgie was about nineteen then but she was very petite and always looked younger than her age. She stood beside the piano, lifted up her eyes and put her best into the song, "I Hope I Don't Intrude," composed by William H. Delehanty of the team of Delehanty and Hengler, the original "Happy Hottentots."

I Hope I Don't Intrude

I'm as happy as the day is long, my mind is never easy,
No matter whether I'm right or wrong, you must not think me rude,—
For love it is the burden of my song, with joy I'm almost crazy,
And if, perchance, I sing or dance, you must not think me rude,
And if, perchance, I sing or dance, I hope I don't intrude.
Chorus
Oh, dear, don't you wish that you were me? (Break)
I feel just as happy as a big bumblebee. (Break)
I was walking by her door, when I heard the music sweet;
My heart with joy filled over, and I could not keep my feet.
So keep the music ringing as it makes me feel so good,
And if I make a little break, you must not think me rude.
And if I make a little break, you must not think me rude.

At a fancy ball the other night, myself and little Daisy,
We kept it up till broad daylight, we felt so awful good.
And Daisy looked so fair and bright, she set the men all crazy,
And when they'd ask her for to dance, she'd say, "I wish I could."
Then I would say in careless way, "I hope I don't intrude."

Blithe and happy be the summer day when I shall wed with Daisy,
Then the merry birds will sing their lay, and wild flowers scent the wood.
Then the cares of life I cast away, my mind shall then be easy,
And one and all, if you will call, we will not treat you rude,
No, if you come to see our home, we'll say you don't intrude.

Next she sang an old favorite of minstrel days, a tear-jerker now almost forgotten, "By the Blue Alsatian Mountains."

By The Blue Alsatian Mountains

By the blue Alsatian mountains, dwelt a maiden young and fair,
Like the careless flowing fountains were the ripples of her hair;
Angel-mild her eyes so winning, angel-bright her happy smile,
When beneath the fountains spinning, you could hear her song the while.
Ade, ade, ade, ade, such songs will pass away,
Tho' the blue Alsatian mountains seem to watch and wait alway.

Chorus
Ade, ade, ade, ade, such songs will pass away,
Tho' the blue Alsatian mountains seem to watch and wait alway.

By the blue Alsatian mountains, came a stranger in the Spring,
And he linger'd by the fountains just to hear the maiden sing;
Just to whisper in the moonlight, words the sweetest she had known,
Just to charm away the hours, till her heart was all his own.
Ade, ade, ade, etc.

By the blue Alsatian mountains, many springtimes bloom'd and pass'd,
And the maiden by the fountains saw she lost her hopes at last;
And she wither'd like a flower that is waiting for the rain;
She will never see the stranger where the fountains fall again.
Ade, ade, ade, etc.

It was during her engagement at Herrman's National in 1880 that Georgie made a hit as a poor, ragged girl, singing songs. At first her mother wouldn't hear of it. Then she said: "All right, but don't say anything to your Dad about it." Georgie asked her mother to come some night to hear her sing. Her hit song had the lines: "Give me a penny, Sir, my father is dead, and though I have no mother——." Then the audience threw pennies onto the stage. The night her mother heard her sing these words, she threw a quarter on the stage—but after the show she asked Georgie to give it back to her!

These entertainments were indoors and only at night, and no admission was charged. The proprietors made their money on the beer sold. There was also a wine room, and the girl waiters would sit down and entertain the men who bought wine. The Bowery population was preponderantly German and Irish in those days. The beer gardens would feature a song act, a dog act, or something else. The music was a piano and violin. Business was good, especially on Saturdays and Sundays. Whole families came to these beer gardens. The children would get pretzels. Beer in steins and sandwiches was the order of the day. The Mills family lived in a little house on Eldridge Street, then a good residential section. Georgie's stint netted her ten dollars a week besides her tips of pennies which amounted to twenty-five or thirty cents a week.

After about two years of beer-garden audiences, Georgie got a booking in Bridgeport, Connecticut, for two weeks with her fare from New York paid. A Mr. Cole had built a theatre by installing a stage and other appurtenances into a little store. It was the only legitimate theatre in that town then. During her engagement there, Georgie stayed at a boarding house, the custom in those days.

But before going on to better things, Georgie Lingard had another two weeks' engagement at the beer gardens. Returning to New York, she got a booking at the Volksgarten, at Pastor's and at the National. Again she sang the sentimental songs, already named, did imitations of little girls and babies, and danced. At the Volks, a woman who sang German songs took a motherly interest in her. Volks featured Harry Woodston comedians, a black-face act, ballad singers, a serio-comic and one or two gymnastic performers. As a wind-up they would all join in a grand finale number. The Volks program overshadowed those of the smaller places.

A STERLING HELPMATE

Her next engagement was with Adam Forepaugh's circus. In its Congress of the Nations, the entire personnel took part. Heading street parades and pageants were the "beauties of all nations," led by "The $10,000 Beauty," winner of a national beauty contest, who rode upon the circus' biggest elephant. Her name was Louise Montague.

Louise was being courted by Adam Forepaugh, Jr. Old Adam was against the match and succeeded in getting rid of Louise. She sued him for the $10,000 prize money.

When Louise Montague left, there was no one to take her place until one day Mr. Forepaugh saw Georgie Lingard feeding milk to the circus' newest baby elephant. The boss told the manager, "I will take that little girl there to take the place of Louise Montague. She is a good deal more beautiful." He lost no time in making her the offer, and she accepted. For the three seasons she stayed with the circus, she rode the elephant in the pageants in town after town. The elephant who had been unruly when driven by others always behaved when Georgie rode as Prize Beauty and as the Princess Lalla Rookh.

In the description of "The Magnificent and Sublime Street Pageant of the Great Forepaugh Show," the romance of Lalla Rookh was told in these words:

In the massive, gorgeous and picturesque after-dark street parade of the Great Forepaugh Show, in combination with P. T. Barnum's Colossal Combination, there will be presented for the first time in this city, a most accurate and beautifully realistic illustration of the charming oriental romance,

LALLA ROOKH, PRINCESS OF DELHI

"Who has not heard of the vale of Cashmere,
With its roses, the brightest that earth ever gave;
Its temples and grottoes, and fountains as clear
As the love-lighted eyes that hang over their waves?
If woman can make the worst wilderness dear,
Think, think, what a heaven she must make of Cashmere."

The Princess, Lalla Rookh, will be personated by The $10,000 Beauty, who will appear seated in a veritable Royal East Indian Howdah, upon the back of a kingly elephant, the largest on this continent, whose embroidered velvet trappings touch the ground; a fair young female slave sits fanning the Princess through the rose-colored veils, with feathers of argus pheasant's wings, and following will be seen her attendants, the Grand Chamberlain, Feramorz, "The Poet," and a troupe of lovely Tartarian and Cashmerean maids of honor. . . .

* * *

Then an accident forced Georgie to take a secondary part in the circus performance. Georgie took the part of the bride in "The Indians' Chase For A Bride," an exciting, melodramatic event in which Indians pursued a stagecoach in which a cowboy's bride was traveling. As the coach turned a sharp corner at breakneck speed, one wheel went into a ditch and the occupants were thrown out. Georgie had a broken wrist, and that ended her career as "the beauty riding the elephant." After that she did nothing but skipping-rope dancing in the concert, in which negro singers, acrobatics and dancing were featured, at an additional charge of 10 cents—25 cents in the big cities.

In the big-top days when Georgie toured and retoured the country with the Forepaugh troupe there was considerable distrust among members within their own organization. She recalls that the circus wagon, the official headquarters of the proprietor, was always stationed right alongside the ticket office to make sure all the money was handed over.

Shortly after Georgie quit the circus, her father died and her mother started a theatrical boarding house on Delancey Street near Christie, an actors' neighborhood, for Maggie Cline lived on the other corner, and Zan Frettie lived nearby.

Tony Pastor knew Georgie when she was playing with hoops. One evening, with wide-eyed, childish curiosity, she approached him and said: "I'd like to go in there and see those pretty girls."

She was carrying a hoople with ribbons on it. Said Tony, "You don't think you can go in with that, do you?" Georgie replied, "You hold it while I go in." And he took care of it while Georgie satisfied her curiosity about the great man's wonderful show business.

After Georgie hit quite a stride as a singer as well as a dancer, she once more approached Tony Pastor and asked him if he'd book her in his theatre, on 14th Street under Tammany Hall. "I'd like to come over and play for you," she said, and succeeded in arousing his interest at once. "Come on in," said Tony, "and I'll have my piano player go over your act with you and see what it amounts to." Georgie did very well. Tony was quite pleased. The act went over great. When he hired her (at twenty-five dollars a week) Pastor remarked: "If your act makes good, maybe we can book you for another week." She stayed on an additional two weeks.

From 1883 to 1888 Georgie Lingard's appearances in New York City were with George E. Homer. At Tony Pastor's 14th Street Theatre, during the week of January 11, 1886, they were billed: "The Brilliant Comedy Sketch Duo, GEORGE HOMER and GEORGIE LINGARD, In their original act, entitled: 'He Said He Would Teach Her How To Skate,' introducing skipping-rope song and dance and burlesque skating, Medley, etc.'" "Our Pleasure Party" was a popular act played by Homer and Lingard.

Georgie was equally famous in the team of Allyn and Lingard.

After her Tony Pastor engagement, she was booked to play roles in Broadway offerings. Then, Miss Lingard went to Boston to play at Dr. Lothrop's Boston Museum, which had a stock company and vaudeville between the acts. Then Dr. Lothrop opened another place on Washington Street, about ten blocks down from there and called it the "World's Museum." He put in parts of "Patience" and everybody who was in the show had to go into the "afterpiece." Georgie also played the part of Buttercup in "Pinafore." The average admission price was 25 cents. In the orchestra they charged about 50 cents. Dr. Lothrop had practiced medicine and late in life went into the theatrical business. He was very kind and fatherly and Miss Lingard enjoyed her stay in Boston very much. On the recommendation of other respected citizens of the community, she was admitted to a first-class boarding house—a real triumph, for in those days getting into a Boston boarding house required unimpeachable references.

It was on this trip to New England in 1890 that Georgie Lingard played on the same bills with George M. Cohan, then a youngster of twelve, at Austin Stone's Museum in Boston and other important vaudeville houses. George's parents did a sketch; Josie, his sister, did a toe dance and some acting; and George played a solo on the violin.

From Boston Georgie Lingard went back again to New York to fill an engagement at Koster & Bial's, on 23rd Street near 6th Avenue. For several seasons she played mostly in New York and New Jersey—getting all the bookings she needed from various agents who charged five per cent commission. When she was in New York she lived at home, but out of town she took quarters with another showgirl with whom she had become acquainted.

By this time, through her triumphs in various competitions, Georgie Lingard had won the unofficial title of Champion Rope-Skipper of America. Lottie Elliot was the Champion Rope-Skipper of England, and managers had to make sure the two girls were not in the same show.

At this time her stage routine was pretty well established. First she did a monologue, dressed up as a little girl and acting the part of a child who had just run away from her mother. Then she did her skipping-rope dance. Next, made up as a little boy, she did another style of skipping-rope dance with a difficult series of tricks.

GEORGENA LINGARD WITH SKIPPING ROPE

Georgie Lingard, Champion Skipping-rope Dancer of America

GEORGIE LINGARD IN THE DAYS OF HER BOWERY TRIUMPHS

Georgie Lingard Swinging Red and Blue Railroad Lanterns in a Dance on a Darkened Stage

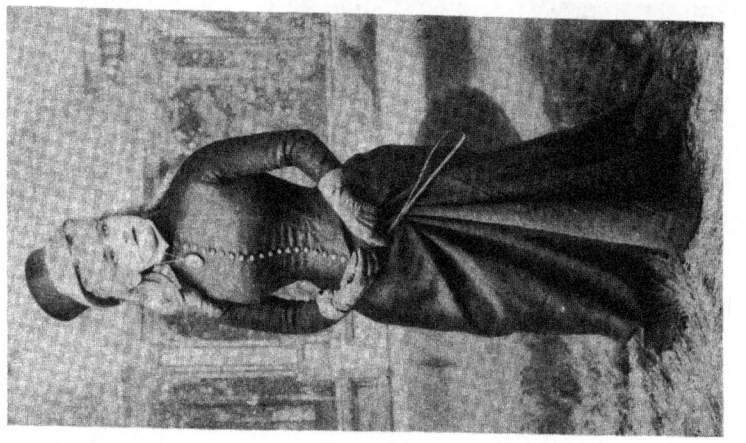

GEORGIE LINGARD IN CHARACTER ROLES

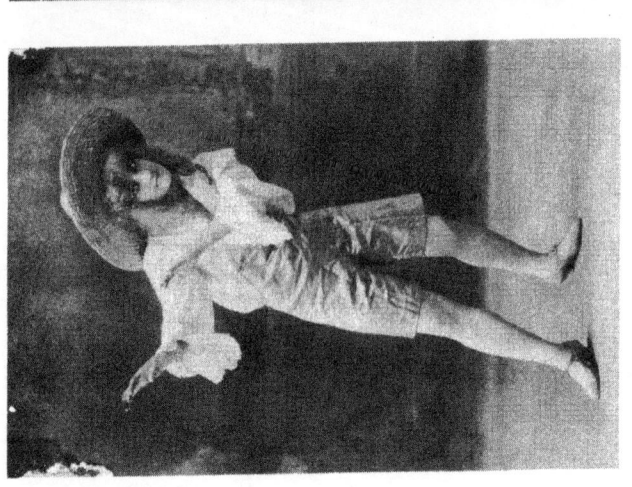

Georgie Lingard in Three Early Roles: "The Essence of Old Virginia," "Little Lord Fauntleroy," the "Flower Girl" Act

Georgie Lingard as Daffy in "Mrs. B. O'Shaughnessy"

GEORGIE LINGARD'S LITTLE LOST GIRL ACT

At the Casino, owned by Sire, The New York Madcaps all did skipping-rope dances and then each one did a specialty. Georgie was asked to join the show to take the place of a little girl who had taken sick. With the New York Madcaps she toured the country for several months. The owner was a specialist in putting on extravaganzas.

At the Bijou Theatre, at 33rd Street and Broadway, in Peter F. Dailey's Company Georgie played "Little Dot," did her specialty, and also played a part in "Country Sport," in which May Irwin sang negro songs.

After the engagement at the Bijou, Peter F. Dailey's Company went on the road and played all the big cities. Georgie again crossed the path of Adam Forepaugh and his circus when Dailey's Company moved into William Harris' Winter Garden just as Forepaugh's Circus completed an engagement there. Georgie's company then played New York for a whole year.

While on the road, being a member of a high-class company, Georgie had to stop at good hotels, but in New York she had a little apartment on Eighth Avenue. Her salary at that time, thirty dollars a week and railroad expenses, was excellent pay for her type of specialty.

The next season Georgie played variety dates in James L. Kernan's theatres in Baltimore, Saratoga, Detroit and other points, and then went back to New York and got an engagement for the next season with George W. Monroe's Stock Company.

Never considering herself a great singer, Georgie depended chiefly on her dancing and rope-skipping. She also did a little variety routine, doing changes such as a little girl talking back to her mother, a child in pretty little dress doing baby scenes and songs. Her comedy was always perfectly clean—she remembers that then people were "very particular," not allowing so much as a "d—n."

She next played the soubrette part of Daffy in "Mrs. B. O'Shaughnessy," written by Edith Ellis, with the heavy comic female impersonator George Monroe playing the part of "Mrs.

O'Shaughnessy." Then she joined Frank Tannehill's company. In the play "Nancy Hanks," a straight, legitimate comedy, his mother played the part of the grandmother and Georgie was the granddaughter. The play went on tour, playing Chase's Theatre in Washington, as well as theatres in Albany, Troy, and points west to California. They played a California theatre for ten weeks in the play "Country Sport," starring Peter Dailey and May Irwin. The tour included a lot of one-night stands with candles for footlights in some Texas theatres.

As to Georgie Lingard's ability to act in children's roles, even after she had reached maturity, this item from the *Dramatic Mirror* of May 1899 is enlightening:

A quaint little story is told of that pretty young New Yorker, Georgie Lingard. She is extremely petite and childlike on the stage, and while playing in Canada she was one day surprised to receive a visit at the hotel from several children. It seemed that they were from wealthy families, and made a point of singling out the child actresses who came to the city to entertain them. They had brought various little juvenile gifts for "little Georgie," and were grievously disappointed to find their ideal shattered even by so charming reality as Miss Lingard.

The latter has been in vaudeville several years, being formerly connected with several noted farce comedy companies with which she played ingenue parts, and introduced her latest dancing specialty, "The Essence of Old Virginia." She made her great success with the famous team of Lingard and Allyn, and is now doing a dainty skipping rope dance, making as pretty a picture as one would care to see with her curls and dimples, and bright girlish face.

* * *

Georgie had known B. F. Keith years before when he was with Adam Forepaugh's Circus, and she wrote him many letters requesting a booking in his theatres. Finally Keith booked her in his little Vine Street Theatre in Philadelphia. On her opening day, Georgie met Mr. Keith and asked him, "Don't you remember me? I was with the Forepaugh Circus? I have written you so many times and I don't understand why I never got bookings from you before. I was with you in the Forepaugh Circus —don't you recall?" But he did not seem at all pleased to be reminded of the old days.

Georgie's spunkiness was displayed when she was playing at this little Keith theatre. After her act was booked, Mr. E. F. Albee, Keith's manager, went to Washington to see Keith on business, and wired the stage manager to let Georgie out. That afternoon, when Georgie appeared to do her act, the stage manager said: "I have a telegram from Mr. Albee telling me to let you out."

The little skipping-rope dancer said, "That's funny, I spoke to Keith and he said how much he liked my act."

Stage Manager: "You will have to quit."

Georgie: "Why?"

The S. M.: "You'll have to change your act before you can ever get another booking here. You can't sing that song here because we have a team singing that same song—and they are headliners."

Georgie: "I haven't any in place of it."

The S. M.: "Well, you can't sing it."

(In Georgie's routine, she carried a basket of bananas on her arm and, as she sang about the fruit being "fresh from the Eyetalian man," she would throw the bananas (one at a time!) into the audience. But the headlining team had a pushcart full of bananas and their vocal effort was likewise on a larger scale.)

Georgie: "I will sing my banana song. It's an important part of my act as I contracted to play it."

Manager: "You will not sing it, and that settles it. Mr. Keith says you are to be closed right now before you go on."

Georgie: "What for?"

Manager: "Because you can't change your song. Mr. Keith phoned from Washington to close your act."

Georgie: "That's not so, because I asked Mr. Keith how he liked my song and he said fine. He said that he knew of the duplication, but that the other act and mine were so far apart that the audience wouldn't mind a repetition."

Manager: "That's my order and you can't go on."

Georgie remembered that Louise Montague retained an attorney named Heveran when she collected $10,000 from Adam Forepaugh. Georgie went to Heveran for advice. He told her to take her costumes, music and whatever other stage paraphernalia was necessary for her act and report at the theatre each day and stand there. "If they don't let you go on, just go back to your dressing room and then go home. They will have to let you play or pay you anyway, because you are engaged for a week. Just stand there until they order you off."

Georgie did just that on Monday, Tuesday and Wednesday. When she arrived at the theatre on Thursday, Mr. Albee, just returned from Washington, came backstage and shouted, "What are you doing here? I told the stage manager to discharge you on Monday. Now look here! I want you to go right out of this theatre or I will have you thrown out!"

Georgie told him, "If you don't play my music, at the end of the week you will pay my salary just the same."

Albee, who had been sitting on a packing box, leaped to the floor, dashed into his office and locked the door.

Her lawyer now advised her: "As soon as we know they won't pay you anything, we will bring suit." But her bookings carried her to California, so that she was unavailable for examinations and hearings and never collected.

She never forgot the incident. Years later, when she recalled it to Mr. Albee, he vowed he had no recollection of the tiff. When she told the story to Mr. Proctor, he said, "You remember it, don't you? Well, you can be sure Albee has never forgotten it."

By the irony of fate Mr. Albee lived to see the day—after

Georgie had become Mrs. F. F. Proctor—when he beseeched and cajoled her to come along on a trip up Long Island Sound aboard Keith's yacht, when Mr. Albee and Mr. Keith were trying to induce Mr. Proctor to pool his holdings with theirs.

At the time when she played Topsy in "Uncle Tom's Cabin" at Proctor's 58th Street Theatre in New York and bringing down the house at every performance, Mr. Proctor first became interested in her. She had written many letters to him asking a booking, but he had never found the need for her act, or possibly had never received her letters.

When we went to see her play Topsy, he had to elbow his way through a very enthusiastic crowd. During the performance, Fred Bond, general stage director of the F. F. Proctor Big Stock Company, leaned over and whispered to Mr. Proctor, "If I could have taken charge of that little girl's career a few years earlier, she could have been developed into one of the country's greatest actresses."

The audience was laughing so loudly at Topsy's antics that Mr. Proctor could not hear what Bond said the first time.

"Look," said Proctor, pointing to one of the other actresses. "She is laughing so hard at Topsy that she can't say her lines."

"That's the way it is," Bond replied. "When Georgie plays Topsy she's so funny that the cast has trouble keeping a straight face."

For the second time in his life Mr. Proctor sat in a theatre and received an inspiration that was to shape his life. The first time he sat spellbound by the performance of the Hanlon Brothers in Boston.

His acquaintance with Georgie Lingard ripened into romance when Frank Tannehill's Company, in which Georgie was playing, appeared with Mr. Proctor's Fifth Avenue Stock Company for two seasons, putting on a different bill each week. Georgie did her specialty or in-between acts. Her act would play "in one." The next entrance would be an act "in two." If a comedian did a "funny," they would have funny advertisements for a backdrop. If it was a "refined" act, they would have a garden background, and the garden backdrop was always used for her solo performances.

Mr. Proctor began sitting in the audience more frequently than his professional interest in the show warranted—and kept asking himself "Why?" If he wanted an act, he simply went and got it. It didn't make any difference whether it was Lillian Russell, Lily Langtry, or a fill-in. He had wanted Georgie Lingard playing in his theatres—he had her there! But still something puzzled him. When Georgie finished her routine, he went back stage and stopped her.

"Miss Lingard, there's something I've meant to tell you before."

"Yes, Mr. Proctor." She smiled.

"I like your act very much. I've always liked your act. Do you know I've been watching you since you were back with Forepaugh's Circus?"

"Thank you, Mr. Proctor. I think it's good, too, but if you did, how is it I never received any replies to my letters asking you for bookings?"

"I don't think I've ever received your letters. I'm afraid that they were filed with some of my routine mail. But I think I'll be able to fix this up."

They had a long talk over the booking, and when they left he took her hand, as if to close the deal, but held it a little longer than was necessary. They had both forgotten their immediate surroundings. Though they spoke only about matters of professional interest, there was a tacit understanding between them about other things.

At the termination of Georgie's appearance at the Fifth Avenue Theatre, she was booked for the entire circuit. Soon afterward she became engaged to Mr. Proctor, and he told her he

A STERLING HELPMATE

didn't want her to be on the stage any more. Not one to be idle, Georgie decided to get some more schooling and enrolled for a year's studies at the Misses Ely's private finishing school on Riverside Drive at 86th Street.

Mr. Proctor, ten years her senior, never discussed marriage plans during their engagement until just before he had all arrangements made. Georgie boarded at the school. Mr. Proctor was living in a house he had purchased near the corner of 34th Street and Seventh Avenue (211 West 34th Street). Mr. Proctor furnished this house entirely, and it became Georgie's first home after her marriage.

On Sundays, Mr. Proctor used to see the Rev. Richard Cobden, the Larchmont rector, and he made all arrangements with him in his quiet way. One fine Sunday he and Georgie paid a social call on Mr. Cobden and toward the end of the visit Mr. Proctor remarked to the minister: "See that young lady—she and I are going to get married when she finishes school."

On the first of June, 1904, Georgie graduated from school, gathered up her things and got them ready to send to her sister in Jersey City. Her niece, who was graduating from the Ely School at the same time, arranged to come over to stay with Georgie in the 34th Street house.

That same day, while Mr. Proctor and Georgie were talking over their plans, he said, "Just wait now, I am going to call Mr. Cobden." He called the minister on the phone and said: "Is this Mr. Cobden? You know what I was talking to you about? Can you get here about 10:30 tomorrow morning?" Mr. Cobden, who had an active sense of humor, replied: "If I have no appointment, I will be there. What do you want to see me about?"

"I am going to be married in the morning," exclaimed Mr. Proctor.

Up to this moment he had discussed no plans with Georgie, so this was all a surprise to her.

The Rev. Mr. Cobden * came down in the morning and they were married in the front parlor, on June 2nd, 1904. Georgie's niece (Ida Willsea) stood up with her, and George Wallen was with Mr. Proctor. He tried to keep the news out of the papers, but on June 3, 1904, the *New York Times*, the *New York Herald* and other papers carried reports of the wedding. The *Herald* ran this account:

> Miss Georgena Mills and Mr. Frederick F. Proctor, a well known theatrical manager, were married in this city yesterday afternoon by the Rev. Richard Cobden, of St. John's Episcopal Church, Larchmont. The bride is a recent graduate of the Misses Ely's School, and comes of an old Knickerbocker family, who were among the early settlers of New York. The ceremony was private. Mr. and Mrs. Proctor last night started on an extended wedding tour, during which they will visit the St. Louis Exposition and later will sail for Europe.
>
> Mr. Proctor has been prominently identified with the theatrical life of New York and other cities for many years. He conducts a chain of vaudeville theatres throughout the East, including four in New York and one in Newark, N. J.
>
> He has been successful in raising continuous vaudeville to a high plane, and has presented many of the most prominent actors and actresses at his houses.

* * *

Right after the wedding, the bride and groom set out in Mr. Proctor's Oldsmobile—a novelty in those days when automobiles were rare. They stayed overnight in a Newark hotel and the next morning visited some of the Proctor theatres.

At about 11 o'clock that same day, as they were driving past a club house in Rahway Mrs. Proctor said that it looked like a

---

* It is an amusing coincidence that Mr. E. F. Albee, a lieutenant of B. F. Keith, later settled in Larchmont, and, though he had been a violent and profane man, became a devout parishioner of the Rev. Dr. Cobden. Occasionally his associates in the theatre still heard him burst into angry profanity, but it is said that his stock remark about any proposal (after his conversion) was "Let us do what the Nazarene would have done."

nice place to stay. Mr. Proctor explained that the club was for members only and he was not a member. A little further down the road were two old ladies riding in a horse-drawn buggy. One of the ladies shouted "Go away, Mister. My horse is afraid of the automobile."

Eager to comply, Mr. Proctor drew his car sharply to the right on what appeared to be a grassy lawn but actually was a ditch hidden by tall grass. The car turned over, pinning Mrs. Proctor in the ditch and throwing Mr. Proctor about twenty-five feet against a tree. He very calmly said, "Put your finger on the button to turn off the electricity." The bride with equal calm shut off the motor. She worked herself partly free and saw that her husband was so pale she feared he was going to die. He said, "Get that robe out, dear, and fix it under my head." She propped him against the tree.

A man in his early twenties, named Kohn, who lived on a beautiful estate nearby, had heard the crash and came down in his car and offered to help. He said, "What's the matter?" Mrs. Proctor said, "That's Mr. Proctor." Then Mr. Kohn's father arrived on the scene. He said: "Mr. Proctor, the theatre man?" Mr. Proctor answered: "Yes. I want to be taken to a hospital." The elder Mr. Kohn said, "No, we'll take you to the club house. We have a doctor there."

So the Proctors did stop at the club house they had passed some few minutes before. It was the Colonia Golf Club.

"We will get a Pennsylvania Railroad doctor," said Mr. Kohn. "He belongs to the club." Two doctors made an examination that revealed that Mr. Proctor had a "Pott's fracture."

The broken bones were pushed back into place and bound up. After five weeks it was discovered that the bones had been set a little to one side. That necessitated breaking the fracture and resetting it.

For this second ordeal Mr. Proctor had to be chloroformed and Mrs. Proctor was permitted to assist and witness the operation. After the resetting, Mr. and Mrs. Proctor stayed at the club an additional two weeks. Again Mr. Proctor tried to keep his personal matters out of the newspapers, but several stories of the accident were published with glowing accounts of his heroism.

From that time on, whenever the Proctors made automobile trips, they always had a man follow their car with a horse, to be ready to tow the car back, because "on almost every trip something would happen to the car." The hired hand would haul the car to a garage, while his employers rode back on the train.

To help in completing his recuperation, Mr. Proctor took a membership in the Colonia Golf Club.

The St. Louis Fair opened when Mr. Proctor was completing his recovery, and they went to the Fair as they had planned, stopping at a nearby hotel and attending the Fair every day for a month.

When Mr. Proctor had fully recovered, he and Mrs. Proctor came back to New York and set up their household at 211 West 34th Street, one of a group of brown-stone houses, about four doors from 7th Avenue.

What Georgie Lingard and F. F. Proctor meant to each other for the quarter century of their marriage can be understood only by those rare life partners who by their own good qualities have realized the full potentialities of marriage.

First in Mrs. Proctor's book of unwritten rules for happy marriage was her principle of acknowledging and respecting the intrinsic worth of the individual human soul—particularly the one with whom she was most closely associated in life. Speaking out of a memory rich with visions of good deeds nobly performed, she asserts that Mr. Proctor was different from any other person she ever met. She never met another person who looked like him, spoke like him, or walked like him.

Secondly, she deliberately dedicated her life to him. Mr. Proctor never permitted anyone to take precedence over her in his love and respect, and he always gave her credit for her con-

A STERLING HELPMATE

structive and praiseworthy deeds. As she sums it up, "I lived for him, and he lived for me. We lived for each other." Fully conscious of the high position he held and had to maintain, she strove at all times to see how helpful she could be to her husband. As a consequence, he continued to prosper, for his abilities and his success were heightened by her helpfulness. The old adage that "Nothing succeeds like success" in this case meant that "Nothing succeeds like a successful marriage."

She was truly "his better half," an ideal confidante, a wife who never crossed her husband nor sought the petty, silly satisfaction of displays of temper, nor desired to win an argument just for the sake of self-assertion.

Mrs. Proctor is still plucky and independent. Recently, when a banker told her that certain payments for properties were not coming in as regularly as expected and that the delinquent purchaser had some petty excuse for withholding prompt payment, she said to the banker: "Tell our man that any time he feels dissatisfied with the deal I'll take back the whole business and run it myself!"

After Mr. Proctor's death, when real estate agents were making an effort to sell the 1200-acre estate at Central Valley, Mrs. Proctor lectured them on how to go about disposing of the choice parcel of property: "If you want to attract a high class buyer for a high class piece of property, do as Mr. Proctor did so successfully. Place a whole page advertisement in the paper. Announce that Proctoria, The Original Proctor estate, is for sale, give all the important facts, and then you'll get a qualified buyer. These little ads, no bigger than my hand, can't get the proper results on such a big proposition."

Mrs. Proctor's pet Pekinese is her constant companion on trips to Europe and when she goes to the theatre. She carries the Peke in a black silk bag and when the lights go out lets her put her head out. One day she did this when a dog act was showing and the Peke started yapping, and an usher came down the aisle and asked Mrs. Proctor to keep the dog quiet. This she did by covering the dog's head again. Once a boy at the theatre door stopped her and said he knew there was a dog in her bag because he could see it breathe. Mrs. Proctor called the manager—an old friend—and told him the boy was very smart and ought to be on Major Bowes' program! The manager put a fatherly arm about the boy's neck and explained to him just who Mrs. Proctor is. She was never bothered again in that theatre.

Mrs. Proctor in her eighties looks back over her fond memories with great satisfaction. From any window of her spacious twenty-fifth floor hotel suite she has an unrivaled view of the entire New York City theatre district immediately below in which she and Mr. Proctor were so active for so many years. The lights (temporarily dimmed in wartime) and the bee-hive activity of the metropolis hold as great a charm for her as ever. As a place of residence she prefers the Park Central to her splendid estate at Central Valley.

A shrewd observer, keenly interested in the world, its people and their doings, she keeps in touch with current affairs, listening to the radio, reading daily newspapers and leading periodicals and attending notable events. She says that the trips throughout the United States and around the world that she enjoyed during the twenty-five years she was Mr. Proctor's constant companion gave her a first-hand knowledge of many parts of the globe now figuring prominently in the news.

And she makes it a point to keep abreast of things theatrical. During a recent interview, she invited her questioner to take time out to listen to a broadcast of George M. Cohan's new song, "For The Flag, For The Home, For The Family." She listened intently, said she thought it a fine song, recognized Cohan's characteristic style, and was reminded of his "Over There."

Mrs. Proctor always has been extremely patriotic. She attributes this to the fact that she was born at the outbreak of the Civil War and the formative years of her life were those steeped in discussions, debates and recriminations concerning the conflict.

"You can't break her courage," remarked one of her old-time

friends recently. Besides her varied charity work and her active interest in her friends and associates, she is putting several grand-nieces through school to prepare them for practical careers. To the shaping of their futures she brings a lifetime of rich experience and wide observation so that they benefit not only by her sponsorship but also by the shrewd judgment, the practical-mindedness and the worldly wisdom of a trouper who plays the game of life most honorably and courageously.

Her annual birthday parties, usually held in West Palm Beach, are events marked for their originality and interest.

A fitting tribute to Mrs. F. F. Proctor was penned on the occasion of her eighty-first birthday by Miss Amy Lyman Phillips, a newspaper correspondent in Florida for more than forty years, thirty of which have been at Palm Beach, where she now represents the *New York Sun* in winter. The poem by Miss Phillips is a spontaneous outpouring of the sentiments of a friend who knows Mrs. Proctor well.

> Greetings, dear friend. And so another year
>   Has rolled around, and finds us all again
> Assembled to do you honor on this day,
>   A bright spot this, in all the world of pain.
>
> What do we love you for? Your faith,
>   Your energy, your indomitable will;
> Your courage, and your love of fellow men,
>   Your cleverness, the beauty you have still.
>
> Here, Liberty stands, enlightening the world;
>   God grant beams from her torch may penetrate
> Far lands, with messages of love and peace;
>   And may our flag, unfurled,
>
> Wave o'er many a happier natal day,
>   And may our ships, so bravely starting forth,
> Deliver safe their cargoes, in those lands,
>   So far—east, west, yea, south and north.

F. F. PROCTOR

We love you for your spirit, gay and free,
    Your histrionic touch; as Uncle Sam,
You welcomed us, your friends of many years,
    Your black eyes sparkling, and full many a Ham

Would give his eyes to play your merry part,
    To sway his audience as you sway your friends,
Making us feel that life's worth living,
    That all the war must come to some good ends.

Of your kind heart and understanding,
    Full many a good song could be sung.
Your loyalty to friendship, your affection,
    Your youth, to which you've clung.

When you stood there, so bravely singing,
    At another memorable birthday night,
You made a lovely figure in your jewels,
    Your lovely little frock of green and white.

Your voice, so true, sweet melody made;
    And it brought tears to many an eye;
Somehow I think that our Creator,
    Could hear it, as it lifted sweet, on high.

It somehow brought to us an inspiration,
    Of perennial youth—that youth that never dies;
The thought came to us, as we sat there,
    That of all present, you were wise.

For somehow, you have left a picture
    That we shall often treasure, when afar;
It is not years that count, when life is ebbing,
    But just remembering how young you are.

So on your birthday, we all greet you,
    And bring our love to you, the greatest gift
That friendship has to offer; and it shines forth,
    Like the sun, when clouds part in a rift.

(END OF ACT 6)

ACT SEVEN

Ring Down the Curtain

One day in March of 1922, a girl reporter from the *New York American* called on Mr. Proctor. Though he was self-effacing, he never had a battery of secretaries to keep people from his office and he was not hard to see. When this young lady entered, he thought she was an actress until she explained:

"Mr. Proctor, I'm here to interview you, and it will really take just a few minutes. The interview will consist of sixteen questions and we are calling it a 'Mental Photo.'"

Mr. Proctor smiled and said, "Let's have your questions, but my answers won't be as interesting now as they would have been years ago when I was a performer."

Certainly his mind was no less alert than it had been when his muscles were more supple and powerful.

In the *New York American* of the next day, March 9, 1922, there appeared the following clues to Proctor the man.

F. F. Proctor, known to thousands of vaudeville fans the nation over, one of the pioneers in vaudeville production, poses for today's mental photo. What do you think of his favorite occupation as revealed in the sixteen questions? Try the list on yourself today.

Your favorite virtue?—LOYALTY.
Your favorite quality in a man?—MORAL COURAGE.
Your favorite quality in a woman?—MODESTY.
Your favorite occupation?—CREATING AMUSEMENT FOR THE MASSES.
Your idea of happiness?—A QUIET DAY ON MY FARM.
Your idea of unhappiness?—FAILURE.
Your favorite color?—BLUE.
Where would you prefer to live?—CENTRAL VALLEY, N. Y.

Your favorite prose author?—ROBERT LOUIS STEVENSON.
Your favorite poet?—LONGFELLOW.
Your favorite painter?—HOPKINSON SMITH.
Your favorite hero in real life?—ABRAHAM LINCOLN.
Your favorite heroine?—JOAN OF ARC.
Your favorite aversion?—HYPOCRISY.
What character in history do you dislike the most?—NERO.
Your favorite motto?—"KEEP PLUGGING."

Among many interesting stories told about Proctor in the twenties, here is one related by M. S. Schlesinger:

I knew Mr. Proctor quite well, and his son, Fred, was a good friend of mine. I remember particularly one experience I had with Mr. Proctor back in 1923, immediately after I had leased the Shubert Theatre (formerly Keeney's) in Newark. Mr. Proctor had a lot where Proctor's Theatre now stands, and he evidently did not want to build at that time and he approached me with a proposition that if I would consent to his playing his vaudeville in my house for the duration of my lease (10 years) he would make me an equal partner in his vaudeville enterprise in the city of Newark. Regretfully I said "No." I was intent on playing the legit in connection with my Broad Street Theatre in that city, having a double franchise—that is, controlling the bookings of both the Shubert and Klaw & Erlanger in that territory. In spite of the fact that the Shubert was very successful during my tenancy, I confess I threw away a real fortune with that "No" I gave to Mr. Proctor at that time. The Proctor theatre there is still a very flourishing institution, while the Shubert, now the Adams, has had a very up-and-down existence, mostly down, since it passed out of my hands in 1933. I am sure that Mr. Proctor had no regrets on going it alone after he had my negative answer.

* * *

The most interesting side of Proctor's life back in his sunset days, his interest in his fellow man, is illustrated by the following quotations from the *New York Morning Telegraph* of October 28, 1921.

GEORGIE LINGARD IN HER TEENS

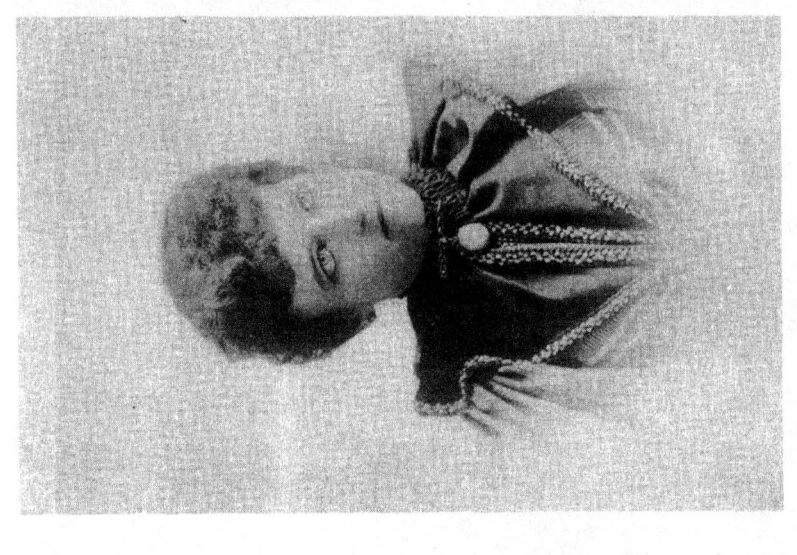
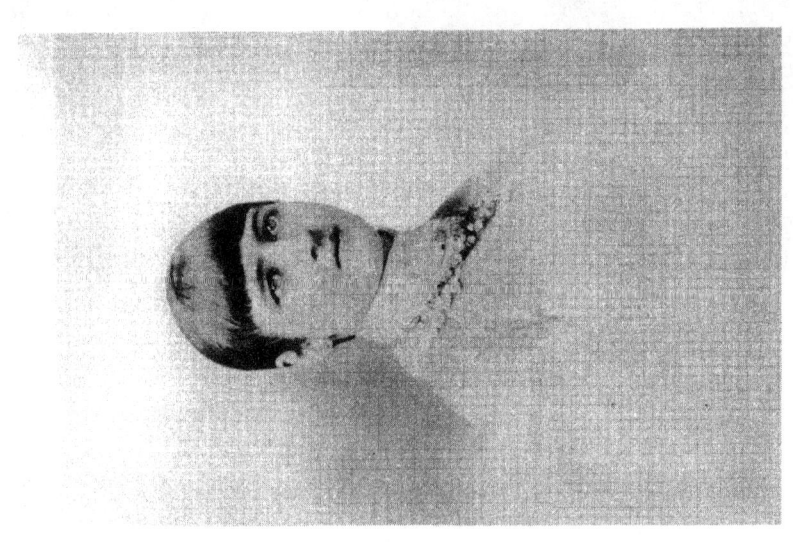

Georgie Lingard in 1876 and 1877

GEORGIE LINGARD AT 21 (IN 1882)

PORTRAIT OF GEORGIE TAKEN FOR HER MOTHER

Mrs. F. F. Proctor (Georgena Mills)

Mrs. Proctor Soon After Her Marriage

Mrs. Proctor, as Uncle Sam, Celebrating her Eightieth Birthday, February 26, 1941, Whitehall Hotel, Palm Beach

MRS. PROCTOR IN 1942

F. F. Proctor, owner of the F. F. Proctor Theatrical Enterprises and vice president of the B. F. Keith Booking Agency, placed under date of October 15 a group life insurance policy upon the lives of all his several hundred employees in his theatres through the East. The insurance is written upon a progressive plan—that is, increasing in amount for length of service as follows:

Six months and less than 1 year	$ 500
One year and less than 2 years	600
Two years and less than 3 years	700
Three years and less than 4 years	800
Four years and less than 5 years	900
Five years and over	1,000

There is no cost whatever to the employee. The insurance is made payable to the employee's own dependent. There is no medical examination.

In addition to payment in the event of death, the insurance includes payment for the full amount of the policy in the event of permanent total disability before reaching 60.

The amount of the group policy placed with the Travelers Insurance Company exceeds half a million dollars and is one of the largest group policies written this year.

The Proctor organization places itself by this action alongside of the leading employers of America who have used a portion of their funds for the purpose of protecting the employees' families against the misfortune of death or permanent total disability.

F. F. Proctor owns and controls 16 theatres located in the following cities in the East: Four in New York City, one in Mt. Vernon, N. Y., one in Yonkers, three in Albany, two in Troy, two in Schenectady, one in Newark, N. J., two in Elizabeth, one in Plainfield. The policy of these theatres is a program of vaudeville and pictures in the majority of the houses, a straight picture policy in four of them, and one theatre is playing a stock company. There are, on an average, seventy persons employed in each performance.

The best known stars in vaudeville, also from the legitimate stage, are found playing this well known theatrical circuit and the photo-plays contracted for by the Proctor management are of the highest class with the greatest stars of the screen appearing in them.

F. F. Proctor has been affiliated in a business way with the B. F. Keith vaudeville and picture industry since 1906, having been one of the founders of the B. F. Keith booking agency. His employees are known through the theatrical profession for their loyalty to their employer, many having worked most of their lives for the organization. There exists a great bond of friendship between this well known theatrical magnate and his people, and this last effort on his behalf to help in the problem of the every-day life of the workers in his theatres and business offices will do much to help cement that bond in the years that are to come, he believes.

* * *

The gratitude of the employees was expressed in a resolution signed by Mr. Proctor's theatre managers, as reported in the *New York American* of December 4, 1921:

The several hundred men and women who represent the working personnel of the F. F. Proctor theatrical enterprises, have extended a vote of thanks in the form of a written resolution to F. F. Proctor, as an expression of gratitude for the recently acquired life insurance policy placed with him for each and every one in his employ. The following resolution, signed for the workers by their chief executives, will afford the outside world some little knowledge of the bond that exists between employer and employee in this great organization, representing sixteen vaudeville and picture theatres located in several of the great cities of the East, including New York, Newark, Elizabeth, Plainfield, Mt. Vernon and Yonkers, in the immediate vicinity. The resolution follows:

"We the undersigned managers of the F. F. Proctor Circuit of Theatres, wish to express in behalf of all attaches of the Proctor houses, our deep appreciation for this latest contribution by Mr. Proctor to their welfare, in providing life insurance for all who have been in his employ for a period of six months or more.

"This is another expression of the interest that Mr. Proctor has always felt for every individual in his employ.

"That each and every one, who contributes to the success of the Proctor enterprises, may continue long to give his best in the Proctor service, is the unanimous purpose of those whom we represent.

"William Quaid, John Buck, Michael Duffy, Dave N. Robinson, Lew R. Golding, Charles Stein, Dan Burns, H. R. Sheridan, John Wallace, Joseph Wallace, John J. Hogan, H. R. Emre, A. J. Gill, Guy Graves, Harry McCormack, Charles Wheland."

* * *

The newspaper libraries contain hundreds of clippings about Mr. Proctor. A large percentage of them do not even give his name correctly. More often than not, these clippings give him the middle name of Francis instead of the correct one, Freeman.* But in all the years that this error was repeated, he never took the trouble to have it corrected. With characteristic modesty, he always told his publicity directors: "Write about my theatres and my shows, and forget about me."

It would require a volume or a set of volumes of encyclopedic proportions to give even a résumé of the newspaper stories about F. F. Proctor. A handful of these clippings have been used in this book to give, at least in outline, some of these press reports. In the hundreds of clippings, there was a preponderance of two kinds of news items: (1) reports on the construction of various Proctor theatres, always the handsomest in a given town, and (2) stories about Mr. Proctor's kindness to underprivileged children, like the following from the *New York Sun* of December 21, 1925:

Twelve hundred children will be entertained by F. F. Proctor in his New York Theatres Thursday, December 24. Through the kind cooperation of the Children's Aid Society, the Proctor management has been able to reach the "kiddies" who attend the schools in the poorer neighborhoods, thus affording entertainment to many who seldom enjoy

---

* Even the usually accurate *Dictionary of American Biography* in its article on Mr. Proctor (by William Bristol Shaw) calls him Frederick *Francis.*

any form of theatrical amusement. The children have been selected from "The Italian School," Hester street; "The West Side School," West Thirty-eighth street; "The Jones Memorial School," East Seventy-third street; the Harlem Boys House, East 127th street, and the Home for Homeless Boys, East 158th street. They will attend Proctor's Fifth Avenue Theatre, Proctor's Fifty-eighth Street Theatre and Proctor's 125th Street Theatre.

* * *

Mr. Proctor and George Wallen were charter members of Albany Lodge of Elks, No. 49, and Mr. Proctor always donated the use of a theatre in Albany to the annual Elks' Lodge of Sorrow benefit, the first Sunday in December.

Striking a rather prophetic note, the following article is another indication of Mr. Proctor's vision. It also shows he believed that vaudeville—in the broad sense in which he always visualized it—would live on. The article, from the *New York Morning Telegraph* of March 18, 1927, is one of the few that he actually signed.

Vaudeville of the future? Not an easy question to answer in this rapidly moving industrial age.

Our continued policy of cleanliness in all vaudeville offerings always comes first in the line of thinking. I sincerely believe that a clean entertainment is the most valuable asset any owner of a theatre can possess, if we may be permitted to speak of entertainment as a possession.

We will cater more and more to the youth of the country during the coming years, and strict attention to wholesome amusement will bring the desired results of continued prosperity.

It will only be a matter of a short time, in my opinion, when the majority of vaudeville actors will assume a more distinct individuality in the minds of the theatre patrons. This will come because of unique ideas presented during the running of their vaudeville acts and because nearly every actor and actress will own their own songs and material especially written for them. This always makes an act more valuable and the intelligent actor is finding this out and is seeking new ideas constantly. The stars are made through this process more rapidly than in any other way.

The revue of the future in vaudeville I believe will run possibly forty to fifty minutes, with a cast of from forty to fifty artists. Costumes and scenery will be even more pretentious than at present and plenty of clean comedy together with feature dancers and ensemble numbers running through as now.

Larger and more beautiful theatres with the necessary accessories will be constantly in the building to house the super-vaudeville of the future.

* * *

The *New York Morning Telegraph* of May 9, 1927, published a story (signed by John O'Connor) about another big Proctor achievement in building "larger and more beautiful theatres."

A new Manhattan vaudeville theatre will open its doors next Monday, located at Lexington avenue and Eighty-sixth street, and to be known as Proctor's 86th Street. It will be the first time in years and years that the Proctor Enterprises has officiated at the opening of one of their own local structures, and it will be the first vaudeville house added to the Keith-Albee booking organization in Manhattan in several seasons.

The new house—to be managed by Herman Whitman, will play six acts of vaudeville with a feature picture and will be the ace house of the Proctor string. Lawrence Golde of the Keith-Albee Vaudeville Exchange will supply the programs. The other vaudeville houses of the Proctor circuit are located in Newark, Mount Vernon and Yonkers, booked by Golde; Albany, Troy and Schenectady, booked by John Daly. The local houses are the Fifth Avenue and new 86th Street, Golde booked, and Proctor's 58th Street and Proctor's 125th Street, booked by Mark Murphy.

The new house represents an investment of $4,000,000, and includes besides the theatre a business block. It was constructed and decorated under the supervision of E. F. Albee, and is patterned after the latter's latest model theatre in Brooklyn. Thomas W. Lamb was the architect. It carries but one balcony, and has a capacity of 3,300. A cooling plant has been installed at a cost of $50,000. A Wurlitzer organ costing a like sum has been added to supply appropriate music for the films shown.

The new theatre will open at 1 P.M., and play continuous, the vaudeville program appearing thrice daily, and four times on Saturday, Sunday and holidays. For the opening program the headline stage feature will be Ned Wayburn's "Promenaders," now at the Hippodrome, and the production which topped the Palace bill last week. The supporting program has not as yet been booked.

This is the second house to be opened by the Proctor circuit recently, the other being in Schenectady, while still another is rapidly nearing completion in New Rochelle.

* * *

Though Mr. Proctor was seventy-six in 1927, when this 86th Street Theatre was opened, he was still alert in acquiring and building theatres. Less than a year before his death, his activity in show business in the New York metropolitan area was indicated by this item in the *Brooklyn Daily Eagle* of December 15, 1928.

F. F. Proctor, who has been a New York manager for over 40 years, will open his new theater at 58th st. and 3d ave., Manhattan, on Tuesday evening. The house will seat over 3,000 and has every modern luxury. It is Spanish in design. The policy will be Keith-Albee vaudeville and motion pictures, run continuously. The new house replaces the magnificent Pleasure Palace erected on the same site about 30 years ago, by Mr. Proctor.

The stage of the old theater originally had no back wall, and the performances could be seen by two audiences, one in the theater and the other seated at tables in the Palm Garden sipping liquid refreshment, or eating hearty dinners. The plan did not work out well, and was finally abandoned. E. D. Price was the first manager, and the house got a most auspicious start under his direction.

Mr. Proctor is still hale and hearty and looks after the details of the half-dozen big houses that bear his name.

The *New York American* six days later, December 21, 1928, added a few more details to the story.

* * *

F. F. Proctor celebrated his fortieth anniversary as a theatrical manager last evening by opening his latest playhouse, the Fifty-eighth Street Theatre. It is built on the site of the one-time Pleasure Palace, which the same magnate dedicated to public amusements thirty-two years ago.

The new Proctor house is a worthy successor of that famous old resort. Its structural note is Spanish and in color and decoration the Iberian art prevails. The approaches through tunnelled lobbies from Lexington avenue and Fifty-eighth street are typical of Spanish corridors and colonnades and the foyer is a patio of Castillian type.

The house is equipped with the latest devices for heating, ventilation, cooling and safety operation. Moreover, it is one of the first theatres to be fitted with the Photophone equipment of the Radio Corporation of America. There is a seating capacity of 3,000.

Last evening's audience was an invited one. The first public performance will be held tonight.

* * *

A guest program commemorating the Inaugural Performance at Proctor's new Fifty-Eighth Street Theatre on December 20, 1928, paid a fitting tribute to the master showman. It was entitled "F. F. Proctor. Outline of Remarkable Career of America's Dean of Theatre Managers Who Marks His Fortieth Anniversary as a Metropolitan Showman With the Opening of This Theatre."

This program said, "The opening of this perfect modern playhouse celebrates the fortieth anniversary of F. F. Proctor as a metropolitan manager and owner of theatres," and it gave a résumé of his career, from the days when he "practised flip-flops, cart wheels, horizontal-bar tumbling and other juvenile feats which appealed to him." It told how "his name was made both on the Variety stage and in the circus" and how "he advanced from ground acrabat and horizontal-bar performer to sensational equilibrist, was engaged for a European tour—the acme of good fortune in those days—and appeared with marked success in most of the famous music halls of England and the continent of Europe."

The program reviewed how he "returned to the United States in 1880 with his savings—both in experience and money—and decided to acquire a theatre of his own and in that year took over the Green Street Theatre in Albany."

The main events of Mr. Proctor's career were summed up on the last page of the guest program in these paragraphs.

Successful, popular and wisely ambitious, he adventured into New York City in 1889 and opened the famous F. F. Proctor's Twenty-third Street Theatre where he presented legitimate dramatic attractions for two seasons before an alliance with Charles Frohman as partner was formed and the historic Frohman Stock Company came into existence. Proctor's Twenty-third Street remained a stock producing house until 1893, many of the illustrious "Frohman stars" making their metropolitan fame upon its stages until Mr. Proctor decided to yield to the urgent demand of the time for refined vaudeville.

From that point on, Mr. Proctor's career has been one of steady building and development with theatres added one by one in the neighborhoods of New York City and scattered throughout New Jersey and New York State until the present influential Proctor chain became a reality.

The opening of Proctor's 58th Street Theatre in 1896 was a sensation of that time and his first theatre in Newark, N. J.; in New Rochelle; 86th St.; in Troy; in Schenectady; in Mt. Vernon; and in Yonkers; and in Harlem and elsewhere, were quickly welcomed in those communities as real civic assets.

At these new theatres of modern vaudeville, Mr. Proctor not only introduced first the policy of continuous performance which is now universally popular, but enlisted on his programs the greatest stars and the foremost attractions that had ever appeared upon the vaudeville

RING DOWN THE CURTAIN 153

stage up to that time. He not only presented established celebrities of drama and opera, but he soon gained profit and fame by his ability to discover and develop new talent of the finest quality. During all the forty years of vicissitude, changes, competition and rivalry which have marked the history of American vaudeville, F. F. Proctor has never failed to lead the procession in discovering and presenting to his public young and exceptionally talented artists but he has also introduced many of the innovations and departures which other Circuits have followed. His theatres, for example, were the first to realize the possibility and importance of motion pictures as a feature of the composite program and the first films shown in America were seen at Proctor houses.

No living factor in modern amusement is more intimately and vitally in touch with his theatre public than is F. F. Proctor whose entire career since boyhood has been devoted, body and soul, brain and brawn, to the service of that public. To them he now offers the newest example of his stewardship as purveyor of wholesome and progressive entertainment always in good taste to every member of every American family.

* * *

These were the years when all the solicitude that he lavished upon his faithful employees all his life came back to comfort him. In the spring of 1929 he became ill and went into semi-retirement. He had built up so strong an organization that he could gradually loosen his grip on affairs, but he still made frequent trips to the theatres on his circuit, usually sitting in a rear orchestra seat to watch his shows.

Millionaire success though he was, Mr. Proctor cared not for high finance. Interlocking directorates were as alien to his direct, personal management methods as a chess game to a new-born infant.

He did not want to set the business world on fire. And he knew when he had enough. Shortly before his retirement, in the face of urgings from several directions that he extend his empire and also "get in on the ground floor" to reap the tremendous fortunes about to be made in motion pictures, he announced that he had made enough money to provide for his comfort and independence and Mrs. Proctor's and for security of his other relatives and many of his faithful employees.

He was essentially a one-man institution. A large institution it was, but still the product primarily of the genius of one man, himself. His trusted associates worked by his side, many of them for nearly half a century. That simple organization of faithful assistants was all he needed.

Capitalists in the banking profession and Wall Street promoters were collaborating on all-out plans to promote the motion picture. Enticing offers of reorganization were made to Mr. Proctor and other owners of extensive chains. Mr. Proctor, for one, turned a deaf ear. One by one, during 1928, he had been selling off various of his holdings, getting good prices. His one concern was to underwrite the security of his loved ones and to provide for the futures of his faithful employees and as many deserving troupers as he could.

In the spring of 1929 he negotiated a sale of his remaining theatres to the Radio-Keith-Orpheum combination, an amalgamation of officials of the Radio Corporation of America and vaudeville officials. The press made due announcement of this last big deal, for example, the *New York Herald Tribune* of May 15, 1929.

> Purchase of the eleven theatres owned by the F. F. Proctor interests and the addition to the nation-wide enterprises of the Radio-Keith-Orpheum Corporation, was announced yesterday by Hiram S. Brown, its president. The sale was closed yesterday, but the theaters will not be taken over until August 1. No details as to the price were revealed.
>
> Mr. Proctor, known as the dean of vaudeville managers, has been active in theatrical work in the metropolitan area for forty years. . . .
>
> The sale of Mr. Proctor's chain of theaters has been caused by the manager's decision to retire from active theatrical work. . . .
>
> The Proctor Theaters taken over by R-K-O include Proctor's new Fifty-Eighth Street Theater, recently opened; the new Proctor Eighty-

sixth Street Theater, Proctor's 125th Street Theater and Proctor's Twenty-Third Street Theater in New York City; also the Proctor's theaters in Newark, Schenectady, Yonkers, New Rochelle, Mt. Vernon, Troy and Albany.

* * *

The *New York Evening World* of the same date ran the following.

Retiring after forty years in the theatrical business, F. F. Proctor today disposed of his holdings to Radio-Keith-Orpheum, which thereby strengthens its chain of nation-wide theatres by thirteen Class A houses in Greater New York, up-State and New Jersey. . . .

F. F. Proctor is the dean of vaudeville managers. . . . He has always maintained a working agreement with B. F. Keith, and now that he has decided to retire he has turned over his theatres to the orgaanization with which he has been so long associated.

* * *

The *New York Times* of the same date carried a lengthy article which estimated the value of the Proctor circuit at sixteen to eighteen million dollars.

Mr. Proctor's ailment, congestion of the lungs, became worse, but mentally he was as active as ever. He was forced to reduce his physical activity to a minimum and had to depend more and more on Mrs. Proctor and the Wallen brothers for the execution of business matters. But he wrote out a 600-page will in his own hand to make sure that not a single relative or associate should be overlooked.

Clarence Wallen and his brother George, after working all through the night of August 10th to clear title to the Proctor properties for the RKO deal, went up to see their chief the next day. Happy that the tough chore of settling the deal was over, he announced: "Now we'll forget all about business and go up to Central Valley and just loaf!" Three weeks later, on September 4, Mr. Proctor died.

The *New York American* of September 5, 1929, published the following obituary of Mr. Proctor:

The "dean of vaudeville" died yesterday at the age of seventy-seven. He had been ill for several months and succumbed to congestion of the lungs. He will be buried Saturday, with funeral services at St. John's Episcopal Church, Larchmont, at 11 o'clock.

Proctor was performer, manager, theatre owner and "big-time" vaudeville magnate. His last chain of theatres was sold recently to the Radio-Keith-Orpheum combination, and he had retired from active life. . . .

Proctor supplied Charles Frohman with the theatre for his first stock company. He also housed the first Klaw & Erlanger show. He was the Proctor of Keith & Proctor, once all-powerful in the vaudeville world. He proved his theory that no attraction was too high-priced for vaudeville by presenting Lillian Russell to his audiences.

Proctor was a native of Dexter, Me., and started on his career when, as a boy, he went to Boston and secured employment as cash boy at $3 a week in a store. . . .

Starting with a small theatre in Albany, he soon acquired a chain and when he combined with B. F. Keith became a partner in one of the biggest theatrical enterprises the world had seen at that time.

Proctor's was one of the three names associated with the development of vaudeville entertainment in the theatre. The others were B. F. Keith, his partner, and Tony Pastor. Proctor trouped with a circus, Keith started with a little museum, and Pastor was one of the greatest of end men when minstrels were in vogue.

Proctor was the originator of the "breakfast" matinee, starting his vaudeville performances at 10 A.M. daily at the Twenty-third Street Theatre.

Proctor's Fifty-eighth Street Theatre witnessed many notable productions. He also had a long lease on the Fifth Avenue Theatre and made it the home of New York's first all-star stock company.

* * *

The reins to the remaining Proctor empire have been transferred; the curtain has dropped on a full, glorious, satisfying life; the obituaries have been published; the name of Proctor has become a legend. Only one more stray item remains to be published in the public prints. Three weeks after his death the newspapers carried details of the disposition of his estate of many millions—his bequests to actors living at the Actors' Fund Home in Englewood, N. J., to The Actors' Fund, to the National Vaudeville Artists, Inc., and to individual associates and employees.

(END OF ACT 7)

ACT EIGHT

Monuments to the Man

SCENE 1. THE PROCTOR EMPIRE
SCENE 2. FAMOUS FIRSTS
SCENE 3. "AS I RECALL . . ."
SCENE 4. THE PRESS

The achievements of Mr. Proctor are summed up in the four divisions of this section—a roster of his theatres, his famous pioneer accomplishments, personal comments of contemporaries, and newspaper editorials.

1. THE PROCTOR EMPIRE

Among Mr. Proctor's more important theatres were the Fifth Avenue, Twenty-Third Street, Fifty-Eighth Street, Eighty-Sixth Street and One Hundred and Twenty-Fifth Street theatres in New York City.

That combination of figures—5-23-58-86-125—is indicative of how systematic and well organized were Mr. Proctor's enterprises. Blanketing the entire theatre district of New York City, they represent a veritable ladder of success. In whatever part of town one happened to be, he was sure to be near a Proctor house offering the world's most renowned artists with the least possible strain on one's purse.

In the order of their coming under the Proctor banner, the following theatres were included in the Proctor chain:

1880   Levantine's Novelty Theatre, Albany, N. Y.
        Green St. between Division & Hamilton Sts.

1884	Martin's Opera House, Albany, N. Y.
	Cor. State & Pearl Sts.
1884	The Theatorium, Rochester, N. Y.
1884	Proctor's Theatre, Amsterdam, N. Y.
1884	Proctor's Opera House, Utica, N. Y.
1886	Proctor's Novelty Theatre, Brooklyn, N. Y.
	Southwest Corner Broadway & Bedford Ave.
1886	Proctor's New Grand Opera House, Boston, Mass.
	Washington St.
1886	Academy of Music, Rochester, N. Y.
1886	H. R. Jacobs' Court Street Theatre, Buffalo, N. Y.
1886	Proctor's Grand Opera House, Syracuse, N. Y.
1886	H. R. Jacobs' Cleveland Theatre, Cleveland, Ohio.
1887	Proctor's Criterion Theatre, Brooklyn, N. Y.
1887	Proctor's Griswold Opera House Theatre, Troy, N. Y.
1888	Proctor's New Haven Opera House, New Haven, Conn.
1888	Proctor's Grand Opera House, Bridgeport, Conn.
1888	Proctor's Opera House, Hartford, Conn.
1889	Proctor's Opera House, Lancaster, Pa.
1889	Proctor's Worcester Theatre, Worcester, Mass.
1889	Proctor's Lynn Theatre, Lynn, Mass.
1889	Proctor's Theatre, Brooklyn, E. D., N. Y.
1889	Proctor's Theatre, Brooklyn, W. D., N. Y.
1889	Proctor's Grand Opera House, Wilmington, Del.
1889	Leland Opera House, Albany, N. Y.
	S. Pearl St., between Beaver St. and Hudson Ave.
1889	Proctor's Twenty-Third Street Theatre, New York City.
	141 W. 23rd St.
1889	Proctor's Albany Theatre, Albany, N. Y.
1890	Jacobs' Lyceum, Philadelphia, Pa.
1894	Amphion Theatre, Brooklyn, N. Y.
	Greenpoint Section.
1895	Proctor's Fifty-Eighth Street Theatre and Open-Air Roof Theatre, New York City.
	Also known as Proctor's Pleasure Palace, 58th St. & 3rd Ave.
1898	Proctor's Newark Theatre, Newark, N. J.
	Park Place, facing Military Park.

F. F. PROCTOR

1900   Proctor's Fifth Avenue Theatre, New York City.
        Broadway & 28th St.
1900   Proctor's 125th Street Theatre, New York City.
        Between Park & Lexington Aves.
1901   Proctor's Theatre, Montreal, Canada.
        Formerly Her Majesty's Theatre.
1904   Albany Annex Theatre, Albany, N. Y.
        N. Pearl St. between Maiden Lane & Steuben St.
1905   Newark Bijou Dream, Newark, N. J.
        Corner Washington St. & Branford Pl.
1905   Proctor's Lyric Theatre, Newark, N. J.
        Market St. near Beaver St.
1905   Proctor's Palace Theatre and Proctor's Palace Roof Theatre, Newark, N. J.
        Market St., between Halsey and Washington Sts.
1907   Proctor's Theatre, Plainfield, N. J.
1907   Proctor's Bijou Dream, Elizabeth, N. J.
        East Jersey St.
1907   Proctor's Broad Street Theatre, Elizabeth, N. J.
1907   Proctor's State Street Theatre, Schenectady, N. Y.
1909   Proctor's Theatre, Cohoes, N. Y.
1909   Plainfield Opera House, Plainfield, N. J.
1909   Proctor's Theatre, Perth Amboy, N. J.
1910   Proctor's Theatre, Port Chester, N. Y.
1912   The Lyceum, Troy, N. Y.
1913   Proctor's Grand Theatre, Albany, N. Y.
        Corner Clinton Ave. & N. Pearl St.
1913   Proctor's Broad Street Theatre, Plainfield, N. Y.
1913   Proctor's Mount Vernon Theatre, Mount Vernon, N. Y.
1915   Proctor's Fourth Street Theatre, Troy, N. Y.
1916   Proctor's Theatre, Yonkers, N. Y.
1919   Proctor's Harmanus Bleecker Hall, Albany, N. Y.
        Washington Ave., So. of Lark St.
1926   Proctor's New Theatre, Schenectady, N. Y.
        432 State St.
1927   Proctor's Eighty-Sixth Street Theatre, New York City.
        86th St. & Lexington Ave.

MR. PROCTOR'S COAT OF ARMS

Arms: Argent, a chevron sable between three martlets, gules.
Crest: A pied greyhound, sejant, collared or.
Motto: Toujours Fidèle.

Interpretation—
Arms: On a silver shield a black chevron between three red swallows.

Crest: A piebald greyhound, seated and wearing a golden collar.
Motto: Always Faithful
Note that the martlets are legless, untiring and never-resting swallows, and the greyhound is another symbol of speed and activity.

PARENTS OF MR. AND MRS. PROCTOR

ABOVE: THOMAS ALPHEUS PROCTOR AND LUCY ANN TUFTS OF DEXTER, MAINE
BELOW: RUBEN CROWELL MILLS AND SARAH HAYES OF NEW YORK CITY

PROCTORIA, THE 1200-ACRE ESTATE AT CENTRAL VALLEY, N. Y.
ABOVE: ENTRANCE.   BELOW: SWIMMING POOL

The Proctor Yachts, "Georgena I" and "Georgena II" (Deck Lounge)

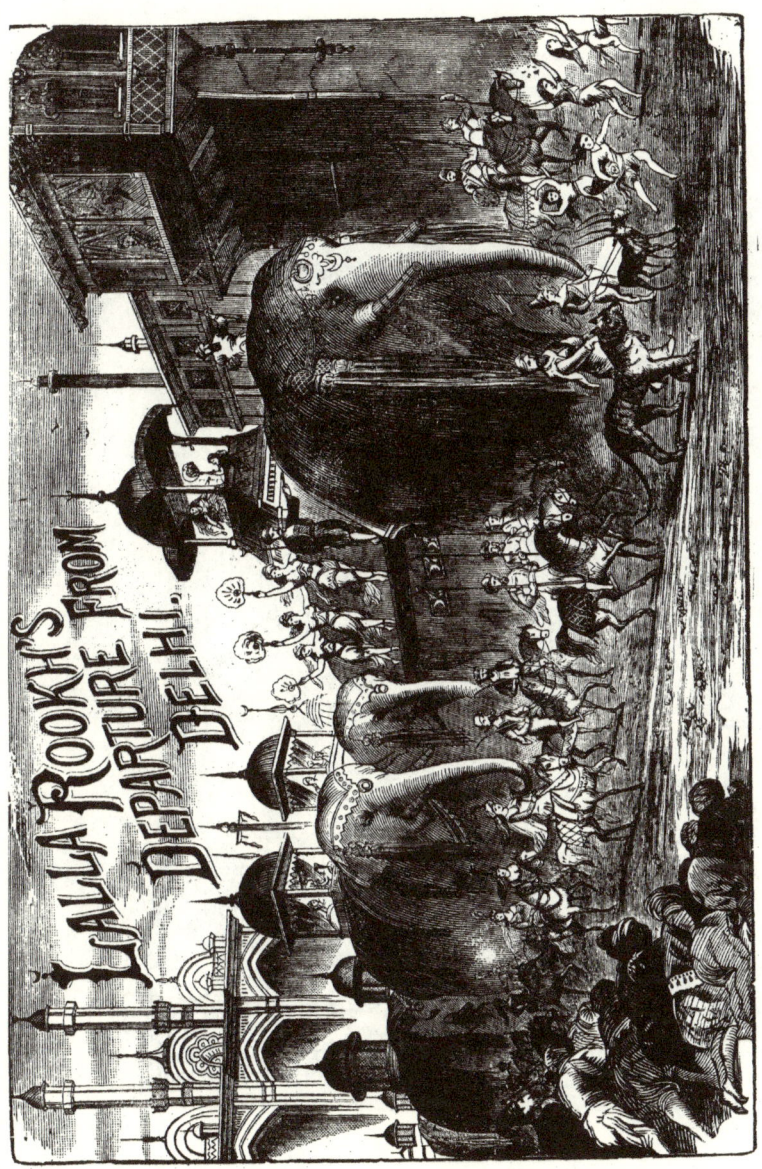

GEORGIE LINGARD SEATED IN HOWDAH ON LEADING ELEPHANT IN THE GREAT FOREPAUGH PARADE

An Audience at Proctor's Pleasure Palace, 1899

F. F. PROCTOR DEAD; DEAN OF VAUDEVILLE

Founded a Chain of Theatres Recently Sold to Radio-Keith-Orpheum Circuit.

GYMNAST OF NOTE AT FIRST

Had to Help Support Family as Boy at Father's Death—Fortune Estimated at $16,000,000.

Frederick Francis Proctor, prominent for more than half a century in New York theatricals and dean of vaudeville managers, died at his home in Larchmont, N. Y., yesterday, at the age of 78 years, after an illness of several months. Death was due to congestion of the lungs.

Mr. Proctor retired from active management last May, at which time he sold his circuit of houses, located in this city and State and in New Jersey, to the Radio-Keith-Orpheum Corporation. Actual control of the theatres changed hands on Aug. 1. While the price Mr. Proctor received for his circuit was not revealed, Broadway estimated it to be around $16,000,000. He planned to take a trip around the world, but failing health prevented.

Mr. Proctor is survived by a widow, formerly Georgena Mills; two daughters, Mrs. Henrietta Proctor Donnell and Mrs. Ellenor Proctor Riley; a brother, Alfred T. Proctor, and a sister, Mrs. Ella Proctor Merrow.

Funeral services will be held on Saturday at 11 A. M. in St. John's Episcopal Church, Larchmont.

Born in Dexter, Me., the son of a country physician, Mr. Proctor when a boy was forced, upon the death of his father, to leave school and contribute to the support of the family. His first job was as errand boy in a Boston dry goods store. At school he had become known as an athlete, and in Boston he continued to practice flip-flops, cartwheels and tumbling in a gymnasium near the store where he worked. His agility attracted the attention of a circus veteran, and it was not long before young Proctor was touring in vaudeville and circuses. He became an equilibrist, and so sensational was his work that he was engaged for a European tour, the height of good fortune in those days. Under the name of Levantine he appeared in all the better known English and continental music halls.

In 1906 Mr. Keith and Mr. Proctor

HERALD-TRIB. SEP 8

, SUNDAY, SEPTE

Proctor Funeral Is Attended by Stage Veterans

Pioneer of Chain Theater and Vaudeville Paid Tribute by an Old Trouper

Services in Larchmont

Former Acrobat of Circus Died at Home Wednesday

Special to the Herald Tribune
LARCHMONT, N. Y., Sept. 7.—Funeral services for Frederick Francis Proctor, chain theater and vaudeville pioneer, were held in St. John's Episcopal Church here today, and were attended by many veterans of the stage, who reviewed the long career of the theater man, which began in the gas lamp days. Mr. Proctor died at his home here Wednesday and was buried in Woodlawn Cemetery.

One of those attending the services was John Le Clair, slender and white haired, who said he was the only living man who played with Proctor when he was a trouper.

Trouper Tells of Early Days

"It was in 1871 that I first met Fred," he said. "We were both playing at L. B. Lent's Circus. My partner and I did

Proctor's 23rd Street Theatre

1928   Proctor's New Rochelle Theatre, New Rochelle, N. Y.
       580 Main St.

* * *

2. MR. PROCTOR'S PIONEER ACCOMPLISHMENTS

Mr. Proctor was too modest a man to be continually claiming credit, and Pat Casey, who stands high in any list of theatrical men, past or present, recently said, "Mr. Proctor probably never gave out three interviews in his life."

Neither Mr. Proctor nor any of his former associates ever claimed he was a pioneer in vaudeville, although those who knew him long and well testify that he was *the* pioneer. Mr. Proctor was too much occupied with treating his fellow man right, putting his own live-and-let-live philosophy into practice, evolving new and better policies for the improvement of his own enterprises and for the benefit of every last individual who worked with him as employee, associate, actor or tradesman.

He never had the desire nor the time to take bows. So, now, his biographers give credit where it is due.

Variety or vaudeville, when Proctor, Keith and others began their respective careers in that form of entertainment, was already an ancient institution. Variety had its roots in circuses and minstrels, and its beginnings are so remote that it would be difficult to trace them accurately. Vaudeville in one form or another, has been an amusement of the people in America and Europe for two or three hundred years.

It was in 1880 that Mr. Proctor leased the Green Street Theatre in Albany and began his career as a manager, and that was five years before his chief rival in vaudeville, B. F. Keith, bought a part interest in the Gaiety Theatre in Boston, though Mr. Keith had already had some experience managing a circus.

Robert Grau, in his book "The Business Man in the Amusement World" (1910, Broadway Publishing Company), in his chapter: "F. F. Proctor, from Acrobat to Vaudeville King" says, ". . . when all is summed up, Mr. Proctor may well lay claim to being 'a' father of the great expansion from 'variety' of the 60's to the vaudeville of today, if indeed he be not 'the' father of it all!"

The labors of Mr. Proctor and other pioneers in variety entertainment made their mark in their time, and even in our time their influence is so strong that it is foolish to talk of the "death of vaudeville."

When it is announced that Amos 'n' Andy have rounded out so many successful years in radio, it should be borne in mind that McIntyre and Heath and other great black-face comedians of an earlier era laid the foundation for such success. When millions thrill to a World's Fair Aquacade that makes a fortune in two seasons, we should not forget that the art which is now so lavishly produced began when Annette Kellermann and other diving Venuses performed in a 30 x 20 x 8-foot tank on a vaudeville stage, with mirrors on three sides. When the Radio City Rockettes, "the world's greatest precision dancers," enrapture some 6,000,000 people a year in New York City, don't forget that the outstanding dancing boys and girls of vaudeville and variety did yeoman service originating and developing this form of entertainment.

Present-day showmen, who are capitalizing handsomely in the amusement field, might well pay homage to the pioneers who created and developed the art and the business of amusement.

Mr. Proctor's early works will live on and bear fruit, "owing to the power which personality in theatrical entertainment has over the public," as Sir Harry Lauder put it.

At ten, twenty and thirty cent admissions, Mr. Proctor and his associate, Henry R. Jacobs, presented star-studded entertainment in the vaudeville, stock and concert fields. Those were the beginnings of Mr. Proctor's life-long policy of furnishing

MONUMENTS TO THE MAN

for the masses the highest class of artists at the most reasonable prices in all show history. Just as in other business fields, the pioneer of lower prices and better quality in amusement earned a fortune for himself by widening his market and benefitting the public.

But we are to remember that Mr. Proctor insisted on quality. In his theatres the show must not be cheap. According to the *New York Sun* obituary, "Mr. Proctor is given credit for elevating vaudeville from the 'ham actor' stage to the high position it holds today, and he accomplished this by splitting with an early partner, who insisted on maintaining the 'ten-twenty-thirty' price while Mr. Proctor believed that the scale should be elevated to 25 cents to $1, thus allowing the producers to engage better talent."

In 1902, he was still considering the financial limitations of the multitudes, and his prices "included a fit for every purse," 25, 35 and 50 cents, reserved seats for 75 cents and box seats for $1, to accommodate those who were willing to pay for advance reservations.

Mr. Proctor was a pioneer in interspersing the best acts in vaudeville with dramatic presentations and combining the whole in the *continuous* performance.

In 1892, the 23rd Street Theatre was New York's first home of continuous vaudeville. Performers began at 11 A.M. and continued uninterruptedly until 11 P.M., and in its day this was considered the leading vaudeville theatre in America.

Mr. Proctor was a night club pioneer in New York City, bringing the idea direct from Europe. In 1896, underneath the "main theatre" of his 58th Street Theatre, he had a theatre-bar-restaurant which was called the Pleasure Palace Café and included two large bars. Entertainers of all kinds did their specialties and there were tables where meals were served to patrons. The place remained open until three o'clock in the morning. The people who attended the main theatre had access to this night club between the acts and after the main theatre's entertainment had ended. With the closing of the main theatre, the night club was also thrown open to the general public. The night club experiment didn't pay and was abandoned after two years. It was probably twenty years too soon, for there was no real growth of night club business until the time of the First World War.

Mr. Proctor set a precedent for elegance in American vaudeville theatres. In 1902 the Proctor Theatre in Newark was admittedly the handsomest theatre in America devoted exclusively to vaudeville.

Mr. Proctor originated the practice of offering the theatregoing public an Early Bird's Matinee—reduced admission rates between the hours of 10 and 11 A.M.—25 cents admitting to all orchestra and balcony seats.

At his Fifth Avenue Theatre he introduced the innovation of having a famous concert artist appear once a week, at 11 o'clock in the morning, one of the most important being Senor Campanini, Metropolitan Opera tenor just from Europe.

As Mr. Leavitt points out, "This was the real start of the big salaries paid to vaudeville people. They may thank Fred Proctor and Austin Fynes, each striving to outdo the other, for the primeval 'boosts.' Proctor hired Campanini and you could hear that silver-voiced tenor for a quarter as soon as you had digested your coffee and rolls of a morning. . . . There is no vaudeville bill to this day, and I say this advisedly, that can equal in strength the programmes put forward at the Keith and Proctor theatres from 1893 to 1900."

Mr. Proctor introduced the policy of securing distinguished stars from the legitimate stage and opera to act in vaudeville performances and the greatest dramatic and operatic artists performed upon his stages for high salaries. In 1906, he offered the famous Carmen, Mme. Calve, first $12,000, and then $20,000 a week to sing at three performances daily.

At the Fifth Avenue, 125th Street and Fifty-Eighth Street theatres, he instituted the new departure of establishing full orchestras.

He was among the first to recognize the value of motion pictures as a feature of composite programs. He was the first theatre man to play a feature picture in a first class theatre when in 1912, at Proctor's Fifth Avenue Theatre he discontinued two-a-day vaudeville to present D. W. Griffith's picture, "Intolerance," a ten-reel spectacular drama showing intolerance through the ages. Another of the pioneer movie bills at this theatre was an episode from "Intolerance," "Judith of Bethulia," in which the star was Blanche Sweet.

He pioneered in furnishing hotel-like accommodations for actors in theatres.

The half-million dollar group insurance policy covering all his employees exemplifies Mr. Proctor's pioneering in the interest of the public welfare.

Mr. Proctor was the first vaudeville manager to conceive the share-profits-with-employees idea and put it into practice. He was the first manager to give his workers an interest in his business. Each house manager received a yearly percentage of the receipts. We have often heard of employees being loyal to their employers. But how seldom we read a press comment like this: "Mr. Proctor was very loyal to his employees with the result that some of his staff were with him for more than thirty years" (forty in fact)!

Always a great believer in the power of advertising, Mr. Proctor started the practice, now widely employed, of listing the various theatres in his chain in box form in one newspaper advertisement, giving the details of the program at each theatre.

3. "As I Recall . . ."

A man is best known by his deeds. Mr. Proctor remembered more than three hundred persons in his will, the members of his own family, all his relatives and their children, his faithful employees, and many needy and deserving people in and out of the theatrical profession. To a pastor in a small New England town, who, Mr. Proctor accidentally learned, was doing a noble work with very limited funds, he gave a life income to carry on his ministrations. Many are the stories of the kindnesses he spread with an open hand wherever he was able to do good, from leaving a quarter of a million dollars to a long faithful employee, to having a clerk slip a five-dollar bill to an actor who obviously needed a new pair of shoes.

The following sincere and grateful expressions are from former associates of Mr. Proctor. They all knew him well. Each has been a great factor in the entertainment world. This is by no means a complete list of witnesses, but it is representative.

As to Mr. Proctor's business ability and financial good sense, probably no more authoritative testimony could be produced than that of the late Mr. Koelsch, who was a Vice President of the Chase National Bank, and who personally handled many of Mr. Proctor's money matters and advised him on his business investments.

William F. H. Koelsch:

"Mr. Proctor had a disposition worth a million dollars," said Mr. Koelsch. "He was a very good listener. He was a modest, retiring, reticent Yankee, *naturally* reticent. Were he to come into this office now, he would likely take that far chair until asked to come over here and sit down. And he was a wonderful student of human nature.

"Mr. Proctor was a man with a heart. His deeds of charity—which were many—he did without kleig lights or publicity. This is another thing he had in common with Mrs. Proctor. She came into this bank recently and withdrew $500, asking for it in five dollar bills, and explaining she was going to spend the day making another trip to an actors' home and wished to give each resident there an envelope containing a five dollar bill—one of her methods of spreading kindness where it is sorely needed. She gets a satisfaction out of this personal, direct succor.

"On many occasions Mr. Proctor would come into the bank and ask for a cashier's check for some sizeable amount. When we asked why his own check wouldn't be good enough, he explained he preferred to give a cashier's check rather than one signed by himself because he wished to give without fanfare wherever he believed the need existed. A man of the opposite type would have let his press agent handle it!

"In Mr. Proctor's day, he and most other successful men looked after their businesses first—and danced afterward. Of course they loved to play just as much as any other young man ever did, but they didn't neglect their business to chase pleasure. In appearance Mr. Proctor was the last man you'd think was in any way connected with show business. You'd think he was a country banker with some two-by-four bank in some small town in Vermont. Mr. George Wallen, for many years one of his most trusted employees, said he always thought Mr. Proctor resembled King George V.

"He was very systematic and conscientious in his business methods. He once showed me a little black vest-pocket notebook, which he used when he made the rounds of his theatres. He would get the receipt figures from each of the local managers and note them in this little book, thus keeping posted at all times on just how each theatre was doing. At the same time he would observe the size of the audience and its response to the show. He would also notice whether the ushers were courteous to the patrons and otherwise diligent in their work. He would drop in unannounced, at any time of day—not as a sleuth, but simply with the desire to look after his business.

"Every dollar that he saved he put into savings banks. When he had accumulated enough in a savings account to pay off a mortgage on one of his properties he would come to the bank and make the deal. One of his strong ambitions was to own his theatre properties free and clear. He once remarked to me, 'I never bought a new theatre until the last one I bought had been paid for.'

"Mrs. Georgena Mills Proctor deserves great credit for the manner in which she encouraged her husband's thrift. She often went to the bank and made the deposits personally to make sure it was attended to. She gave every encouragement to his plan of buying new theatres out of the profits earned on other theatres.

"He borrowed very seldom. He had a big batch of savings bank books. The only reason he would borrow was for the purpose of paying off a mortgage on one of his theatre properties. For instance, in the case of Harmanus Bleecker Hall in Albany, he owned the real estate outright, which was very unusual in show business in those days. He put his money into nothing but his own properties—also a very rare practise for a theatrical man of that period.

"He was one of the original stockholders of the New Netherlands Bank. It was for years the only stock he owned outside investments in his own enterprises. This bank stock he held the rest of his life.

"In his theatre transactions, he was the type of man who, as the saying goes, 'never sold the first thing he bought,' and got rich in the process. In a sense, he never did actually sell a theatre property outright, because when he 'sold' one of his theatres he always took a first mortgage on that same property as part payment—such was his confidence in the soundness of the theatre property he sometimes saw fit to transfer. Occasionally these property transfers were made for reasons of efficiency—as in the case of the Montreal theatre which he operated for a while and then decided it was too far from his regular circuit to fit into his plans as advantageously as a theatre within easier access.

"Here's another instance to demonstrate his thrift habits. He opened his first savings account while he was still a boy, with the famous old Boston Penny Savings Bank, established in 1861 and still in existence. He once told me he had such pride in that first little account that he would never close it as long as he lived. And he never did.

"When high-pressure promoters came to him with their plans and schemes, he measured their propositions with that very reliable yardstick—his own experience. That was a test he had learned to apply in his struggle for success. It was a test he didn't take out of some book. He was brought up in the school of experience and it put him in good stead.

"I recall when he was preparing his will how he would go over it for hours at night, not turning that important task over to someone else. He strove in that voluminous document to be just to all those who were good to him during his lifetime. He provided amply for all those near and dear to him as well as for more than a hundred others he deemed deserving or in need. Many of his employees worked for him as long as forty years. If any employee had any family trouble, he'd want to

MONUMENTS TO THE MAN

know about it. Enough rain fell in Mr. Proctor's own life to enable him to sympathize with his fellow men in their dilemmas.

"Mr. Proctor was never known to hurt anyone's feelings. I don't believe he had an enemy in the world, and I don't believe anybody would have said a bad word about him.

"He would have made a success at anything. He would have been a good banker, a good merchant—a good anything—because he had a good mind, a good clean mind."

* * *

Clarence Wallen:

"Mr. Proctor was a very shrewd man, but *never a trickster*. He was very modest—never went in for self-advertising. He always dodged every function where he might be required to get up and make a speech. He was always very courteous to his employees—genuinely polite, kind and considerate. First thing each day, when he came into the office, he'd hang up his coat and hat and walk through the office and say 'Good morning' to the employees. He was never upstage; always was willing to talk and get anyone's opinion. He would call in his managers and talk to them freely. Perhaps that is one of the reasons he knew his business from A to Z.

"He never dabbled in politics. In business, he was willing to take a chance, and always said: 'If I make mistakes in business, they are my mistakes, and I have to pay for them. I don't expect anybody else to pay for them.' He always kept his word. He was conservative, yet he had a sort of daring characteristic when in his judgment a proposition looked good.

"He was always immaculately attired and his diction was soft and distinct. That was his personal efficiency. In business, he always urged us to keep our desks clear.

"I started with him when I was thirteen, and remained with him for forty years. My brothers, Harry and George, worked with him forty-three and forty-six years, respectively.

"An instance demonstrating his strict integrity comes readily to mind. Mr. Proctor had decided to build two magnificent theatres in 1929, shortly before his death. He planned one in Schenectady and the other on 86th Street in New York city, to cost $1,500,000 and $3,000,000, respectively. He was unwilling to mortgage any of his other theatres to raise the cash for these constructions, so he instructed me to see one of his bankers and negotiate loans to finance the projects.

"Carrying out Mr. Proctor's instructions, I went down to the New Netherlands Bank (now a branch of the Chase National Bank) and told the bank officer that Mr. Proctor wanted to build these theatres and, to avoid mortgaging any of the other properties, he wanted to borrow money from his bank. The officer wanted to know at once how much we'd like to borrow. I told him what Mr. Proctor told me—as much as we may need. I told him, furthermore, that before touching any money that he might loan us, we intended to spend the $500,000 we had on deposit with his bank. He said that was a bit unusual, but asked again about how much we'd need. I told him again what Mr. Proctor told me—perhaps $600,000, perhaps more or less. I also explained that Mr. Proctor didn't wish to take it all at once but preferred to draw on his bank for whatever amounts he needed during the course of the constructions, and whenever he needed the money. The officer promised that he would call a meeting of the directors to pass on the matter.

"Shortly afterward, I was called into the bank and saw the same officer. He said he had been empowered by the board to give Mr. Proctor whatever he wanted. His next question was: 'How much do you intend to pay for the loan of this money?' I said: 'I should say 4½ per cent.' 'All right,' he replied, 'you shall have it at 4½ per cent.'

"Some time later, when our accounting firm went over our books, the examiner came across this loan and exclaimed: 'How do you do it? I've audited the books of some of the biggest firms in the country, and I've never seen the equal of that deal. From 6 per cent to 8 per cent is usually paid for such a loan.'

"I replied simply and truthfully: 'Mr. Proctor's integrity is the answer. He pays his bills.'

"Mr. Proctor was most fair and generous. And he demanded of himself the same devotion to duty which he expected from his workers. I remember a case to illustrate.

"One Sunday night in the summer of 1896, he called the theatre from his home at Larchmont to ask about the business and, in the course of the conversation, he said that he'd been thinking about the morning attendance at the theatres which had fallen off. He made a suggestion:

"'Clarence,' he said, 'what would you think of this idea? Suppose we were to lower the price of admission every morning for the first hour from 50 cents to 25 cents.'

"Mr. Proctor continued: 'That would have a tendency to increase the attendance and make the early show go over better.'

"I told him I thought the idea was a good one.

"He said: 'All right, we'll go ahead with it, but take it up with George.'

"I replied: 'I'll ask him what he thinks about it.'

"Next morning, Mr. Proctor and my brother George got down to the theatre before I arrived. Mr. Proctor greeted him and asked him what he thought of the idea I had outlined to him last night.

"'What idea?' asked George, rather surprised.

"Mr. Proctor wanted to know whether I hadn't discussed with George the idea of reducing the admissions between 10 and 11 A.M. each day, to draw more people in the morning and also relieve pressure of attendance at the night shows.

"George answered: 'I haven't seen Clarence.'

"A short while after this conversation ended, I appeared on the scene. 'Clarence, I thought you were going to talk to George last night,' began Mr. Proctor, 'about the reduced morning prices.'

"'I didn't see him around, Mr. Proctor,' I alibied.

"'Clarence, you should have seen him if you had to stay up all night to do it. I may be at home during the day, but believe me I'm working just as hard as you.'

"He was right, and it was just another lesson I learned from a great taskmaster. And that is how the early birds' matinee started.

"I recall another talking-to he gave me. A contractor, who was doing some work on one of the Proctor theatres in the suburbs, called me up at the 23rd Street Theatre and asked me if it would be possible for me to send him an advance payment on his contract—he said he had certain bills he was anxious to pay on the coming Saturday. I told him that I could and, after finding out his requirements, I told him I'd put a check for the amount in the mail the next day. The following

Monday morning, Mr. Proctor came down to the theatre office bright and early, before I got there. Opening the mail, he found a letter from the contractor in which the latter stated that he was rather disappointed in not having received the advance payment after he had counted on it.

"When I arrived at the office Mr. Proctor asked me, 'Why didn't you send the check?' My answer was, 'We didn't have the money to spare.' (In any week that a theatre operated at a loss, the main office would send a check to make up the week's deficit; on the other hand, whenever a week showed a profit, a check was sent to the main office.) I explained that, because the receipts for the current week weren't up to par and I desired to make a good showing at the central office, I did not send the payment as promised.

"Mr. Proctor then sat down and gave me a brief, gentle but firm talking-to. 'You're still quite young and I'm giving you this lecture to impress upon you the value of a promise. Never, never make a promise in my name or in the name of the Proctor organization unless you live up to it 100 per cent. A promise made for me must be kept!' He ordered that a letter of apology and the promised check be dispatched to the contractor with all possible haste. He then, once more, emphasized that as long as I was in his employ, I was not to make any promise on his behalf or on his account unless I kept that promise. He said he did not wish to have people writing him letters saying they were embarrassed because of promises made and not kept.

"When he was about to buy a theatre, he'd make a price and wouldn't haggle about it. He'd want the easiest terms, but always had a proviso in the agreement permitting him to pay off the whole debt earlier than called for in the stipulated terms. For instance, he'd buy a theatre for $300,000. He'd pay $50,000 down and enter into an agreement to pay the small amount of $10,000 a year on account of the principal and mortgage, but always including the proposition that he could pay a larger sum at any time, or pay the whole debt off at any earlier date than called for by the contract. His purpose in binding himself only to making the smaller payments was so that he'd never get himself in a hole, regardless of the eventualities.

"I have to smile when I recall the incident about the telephones. He dropped into the central accounting office one day and thought he'd make a phone call. Looking about the office, he noticed about twenty-five desks with telephones. Looking more closely he noticed that almost every one of them was in use by clerks. He decided to wait until one of the phones was free, rather than to ask one of the workers to relinquish his instrument. While waiting, he thought he'd inquire about some of our methods of work and he asked, 'Why are all these telephones around here—and all in constant use?'

"I explained that each theatre in the circuit made a daily and weekly report to the central accounting office, and the many clerks and accountants there had to check all these statements, because not infrequently errors were made and had to be straightened out. I told him that if theatre managers didn't make occasional—even frequent—mistakes, we could just take their statements and use them as actual records and statements of fact. He still couldn't understand why there were all these errors. I said, 'They do make mistakes, Mr. Proctor.' He replied: 'Well, I don't think much of the idea. A mistake once—Yes! A mistake twice—well, maybe—possibly. But three times! Oh, no! No, No!'

"Mr. Proctor always paid his managers very well, and always paid them a bonus at the end of the year, based upon the net profit of the theatres. Most of Mr. Proctor's managers started with him as boys and worked their ways up with him. And he made ample provision for them in his will.

"My brother George and myself worked all day on August 10, 1929, and until 3 o'clock the next morning, working on the clearing of the title to his properties to RKO. After a few hours rest, we went up to turn all the papers over to Mr. Proctor. Mr. Proctor was quite relieved that the arduous task of settling the deal was finally at an end. He said: 'Well, now, Clarence, we've got this deal closed and we are no longer operating theatres. Now we'll forget all about business and go up to Central Valley and just loaf!' In less than a month he had passed away."

* * *

J. J. Murdock:

"Mr. Proctor was a quiet gentleman, nothing blow-hard about him. The typical showman, according to the popular imagination, is loudmouthed, like the spieler in front of a circus. Mr. Proctor was none of that. He was very soft-voiced, didn't get excited. Never swore, and he didn't want to hear it from his officials, staff members and general employees. It was drilled into them. Whether managers, treasurers or bookkeepers, they maintained more or less the same tone as he did. He never lost his temper, was always on an even keel. You never saw his name in the paper about the great kindnesses he performed, yet he was doing something for somebody all the time. His whole life was that same way—quiet, apparently, but effective.

"Mr. Proctor would rather have to walk twenty miles and back than to be interviewed. He always wanted to be in the background looking on—never wanted to be out front. He was a gentleman and never a four-flusher. If it became necessary to reprimand an employee, he'd do it gently. He'd put himself in the erring employee's spot and say softly, 'I wouldn't do that if I were you.' Then he'd go on and tell him a little story explaining why. As a result, the trespasser, while not feeling that he was being scolded, would take the lesson to heart.

"He trained himself to understand that he could get just as much out of people without hurting them. All his key men were with him for years. His men were never afraid to say they had made a mistake. All he wanted from them was that they'd learn a lesson from their mistake and set about rectifying it. He was so quiet that you'd think anybody could walk over him. But nothing could be further from the truth.

"He was one of the strictest fighters for rights of anybody I knew, and I came into contact with all of them. I don't know that I ever in my life had a piece of paper from him guaranteeing that he would do so and so. I settled all the labor disputes for all of the different circuits, and bear in mind I wasn't connected with them financially. We became good friends. After settling a case, all I had to do with him was to tell him what I had done and agreed upon, and it was always a case of 'That's fine, John, that's fine.' There was never any agreement, and it wasn't necessary to get his signature to any agreement. His word was always good; he made it good. I had every reason to know that, for many, many times I had nothing but his word.

"He was one of the first to recognize the fact that quick sales and small profit—or in other words, cheap prices for standard shows—should be the aim of a leading merchant in public entertainment. And it was that aim which he so successfully carried out. He wouldn't take a theatre unless it had the capacity so that he could sell the show at cheap admission prices. That was one of his main successes. Therefore he catered to the masses, which covers all standards.

"I did a great deal of business with him. I don't think anybody living had more dealings with him. If you made an honest mistake with him, he'd just say, 'Now, let's forget that and watch out for the next time.' He was keen, bright, right up to the very last.

"There is so much constructive and inspiring stuff to be written about Mr. Proctor's life that a biography of him need have little or nothing about anyone else. But, in Mrs. Proctor, whom I have known for many years, he had a real companion who was always a help to him. There are times in the lives of all business men when they have troubles—strikes for example. All men have worry sometimes. In Mr. Proctor's periods of trouble, Mrs. Proctor was a great help to him. In her presence, he could think out loud, which was infinitely better than trying to keep his problems to himself. He could talk matters over with her, and she was a good pal to him. This is not flattery, for Mrs. Proctor deserves this praise. She has a keen brain. She is smarter than two thirds of the men. And you can't break her courage.

"As to vaudeville, it didn't die out or tire the public. It was in its prime. But when those who built it up from the beginning, through meeting old age and desiring to retire, sold the business to Wall Street, Wall Street fired all the men who were capable of running the business to put in what was termed 'valuable friends.' They believed that Johnny Comelately could run it better than the people who built the business. Wall Street bought it because the earnings were big, and immediately after they came into control of the properties they put in pictures and cut out vaudeville; put in friends who had no knowledge of the business and, by getting outside advice, they dispersed vaudeville and went into pictures. Take for instance a case in Cleveland. The manager of the main vaudeville house there was sent a movie trailer by the new interests and was told to run it. The trailer read, 'This house is going to run all the high class motion pictures,' etc.—all about motion pictures. The manager wrote to the motion picture company headquarters in New York calling attention to the omission of any reference to vaudeville. He suggested the addition of some wordage to the effect that 'This house will also continue the presentation of the same high class vaudeville as heretofore.'

"Two days later, a man called on the Ohio manager in his office with a letter from headquarters in New York telling him that he was relieved of all responsibility for the house and that he was to turn the keys and everything over to this caller.

"It was the bankers who bought out vaudeville, not the picture people. And the bankers bought themselves into the picture business. The bankers knew nothing about pictures or vaudeville or anything else connected with show business. That's how vaudeville 'died' and pictures tried to take its place."

* * *

Mrs. Gertrude Mansfield Wilbur:

"Born of Yankee stock in Dexter, Maine, Frederick Freeman Proctor, owner of the F. F. Proctor Circuit of Vaudeville and Picture Theatres in and around New York, started upon his career at a very tender age, caused by the sudden death of his father which left a mother and five children with the problem of a livelihood to earn.

"Young Fred Proctor left school and secured employment in Boston, Mass., as an errand boy with R. H. White and Company, at that time one of the few large department stores in the U. S. A. Having always been fond of athletics, which in those days had a limited outlet, Proctor was a constant visitor at a nearby gymnasium. It was while practising flip-flops and stunts in the gym that this hard working youngster was discovered by an older man, a professional who suggested a partnership and tryout in the show business. The idea was eagerly accepted by Proctor, and in a few weeks he was launched upon his theatrical career.

"For some years Mr. Proctor worked with partners both on the Variety stage and in the Circus, as a ground acrobat and later as an equilibrist. Then followed the great adventure of a European trip which meant much in early seventies, and upon securing work abroad, Mr. Proctor toured all the European cities of any size, appearing successfully in their Music Halls. Upon returning to this country, this enterprising young man decided to open one of his own, and in 1880 we find Mr. Proctor owning, operating and appearing in his theatre, known as the Green Street, in Albany, New York.

"In 1889 Mr. Proctor went to New York and opened Proctor's Twenty-third Street Theatre which was built especially for him. Legitimate productions were presented at this house for a couple of seasons and then Mr. Proctor and Charles Frohman formed a partnership and the Frohman Stock Company came into existence. Here many of the Frohman stars first made their appearance, including Maude Adams, Douglas Fairbanks, Viola Allen, Lionel Barrymore, William Courtney, Allison Skipworth, Frances Starr, Charles Richmond, Fay Bainter and many others. The theatre remained a production house until 1893, when Mr. Proctor, who always kept abreast of the times, installed a policy of continuous vaudeville, opening the theatre at 10:00 A.M. and closing at 11:00 P.M. This was something very new to New York, and was successful from the start.

"The greatest stars that vaudeville had ever known appeared at this theatre at this time. From this beginning started the F. F. Proctor Circuit of Theatres which continued to grow and prosper with houses located in and around New York City, in up-state New York, and New Jersey. Mr. Proctor's slogan was 'Good Clean Entertainment for Women and Children at Popular Prices' and it paid. Brought up in an honest home environment, Proctor grasped the idea very early in his business career that if one would be successful in his line he should make a bid for the patronage of the women and children and so for forty-five years this quiet, unobtrusive worker made a study of how to please the women and children by offering special inducements to secure their constant attendance, deciding that if the ladies and youngsters visit a showhouse, the men are very likely to follow. The result of this continued effort in one direction drew a steady patronage of the family element to the numerous playhouses bearing the owner's name. These home folk acquired the habit of visiting Proctor's once or twice a week, at the same time passing the idea on to their youngsters.

"Mr. Proctor could always be found at his desk during the working days of the week, unless out of town upon a tour of inspection of his theatre holdings, and evinced the same interest in the work after he became a millionaire, that he did when there was only one tiny theatre to engage his attention. At that time the theatre seated about three hundred persons and later Mr. Proctor catered to approximately forty thousand.

"Mr. Proctor was honest and insisted that all bills be paid the first of the month. When a manager tried to cover up unpaid bills so as to make a good showing as to receipts, he got into serious trouble with the 'boss.'

"Mr. Proctor had a very clean name morally, something unusual in the life of a man so prominent in the theatrical world. He was loyal to those who worked for him to a marked degree, and this thought followed them long after he passed on, for many members of his working family were mentioned in his will in a most generous fashion; in fact Mr. Proctor's will made the pages of every New York paper at the time of his death because of his generosity shown therein to his workers.

"Mr. Proctor liked good, clever, clean entertainment and abhorred filth. He had been frequently seen walking out of one of his houses when an act resorted to dirt for its success. He was a very modest man; never sought the limelight; in fact, disliked it exceedingly. He informed his press agent at one time to advertise the theatres, to play *them* up and forget him entirely.

"In my nineteen years in Mr. Proctor's employ, I never heard him use profanity, and seldom witnessed any expression of anger. Because of the qualities of character above mentioned he endeared himself to his office staff and they repaid his loyalty to them with a strong desire to please him in every way possible and respected him highly.

"My father, George E. Mansfield of Boston, Mass., and Mr. Proctor were partners * seventy-five years ago, and the family always remained friends although the partnership was severed after a few years.

"Mr. Proctor had a remarkable memory. His employees had to be very careful always to tell the truth when talking with him because he could remember what happened forty years ago or yesterday.

"During this man's life he received the respect of the newspaper world and the public in general because he did not depend on fanfare for success but delivered the goods at a moderate price. At his death he received more recognition than any of his better known associates."

* * *

* The Levantine Brothers.

MONUMENTS TO THE MAN

George Kupfrian:

"I first met F. F. Proctor in the early spring of 1900, when he and George Wallen, his Treasurer, came to New York City from Albany to open the 23rd Street Proctor's. Mr. Proctor had a splendid personality, friendly, kindly and generous. He was a great man in his line of business and was loved by all who knew him."

* * *

Hiram S. Brown, president of the RKO Corporation:

"The passing of F. F. Proctor is a distinct loss to the theatre. In the East, where his half-century of unselfish service to his theatres and to his patrons was confined, he was an outstanding figure. He was always a stanch advocate of wholesome entertainment, and the theatres he has left are a heritage to amusement lovers of the communities he served with so much energy and devotion. These theatres are now a part of the Radio-Keith-Orpheum system, and we assume the great obligation of conducting and operating them in such a way that the traditions and influence of the founder of the circuit will be carried on. Mr. Proctor built his entire circuit of a wholesome structure; his name was internationally respected and he made a worthy contribution to the amusement industry of America."

* * *

E. F. Albee, director of the RKO Corporation:

"He commenced the show business from the ground and fought his way through all the difficulties of a small beginning to his place as one of the great showmen of the country. He was a man of integrity and high-mindedness and a showman of rare ability. He was kindly and charitable. His passing will be a distinct loss to the theatrical profession and a great personal loss to his friends and associates."

* * *

Robert Campbell:

"F. F. Proctor was a Life Member of the Actors' Fund of America and he left the Actors' Fund $50,000. Mrs. Proctor has always taken a real, active interest in this old time theatrical charity, being a constant visitor at the Actors' Fund Home at 155 Hudson Avenue, Englewood, New Jersey.

"The first knowledge I have of Mr. Proctor was as a member of the firm of Jacobs and Proctor when they were managing in Albany, New York, what I believe to be the first cheap price theatre in the United States playing dramatic attractions at a scale of prices ten, twenty, and thirty cents, with a few seats at fifty cents. This was some time in the very early eighties, and it was not long after that they added theatre by theatre until they had a very successful circuit of theatres devoted to the same policy. Eventually Jacobs and Proctor separated, but both of them however continued to manage popular price theatres in principal cities.

"The first time I ever met Mr. Proctor personally was in 1893 while playing an engagement at his Novelty Theatre at 4th and Driggs Avenue, Brooklyn, E. D. As I remember him he was one of the most affable and jovial men connected with the theatrical business.

"It was about 1889, I believe, that he rebuilt what had been known as the 23rd Street Theatre on West 23rd Street between 6th and 7th Avenue, into what became known as Proctor's 23rd Street Theatre. This house was immediately successfully established as a first-class theatre in New York and was opened with Neil Burgess in the original production of Charles Bernard's play 'The County Fair.'

"Soon after that time Mr. Proctor entered into an arrangement with Charles Frohman for the establishment of the Frohman Stock Company in this theatre, where it remained until 1893 when it was moved into a new theatre built for Frohman by Al Hayman and Frank W. Sanger, the Empire Theatre."

* * *

Louis R. Golding:

"I came to work for Mr. Proctor in 1908 when his offices were in the old Putnam Building now replaced by the Paramount Theatre Building. I came in as an office boy for his son, F. F. Proctor, Jr., who was the general manager of the Proctor circuit embracing theatres in New York, Albany, Troy, Schenectady, Newark, Elizabeth and Perth Amboy.

"At the Proctor 23rd St. Theatre he introduced an innovation once a week in the morning at 11:00 A.M. by having a famous concert artist appear; one of the more important as I remember being Senor Campanini who came from Europe to sing in the Metropolitan.

"Regardless of anything said to the contrary, he was the first theatre man to play a feature picture in a first class theatre when in 1912 at Proctor's 5th Ave. Theatre he discontinued two-a-day vaudeville to present D. W. Griffith's feature picture, 'Intolerance,' a ten-reel spectacular drama showing intolerance through the ages. Later, this picture was broken up and an excerpt taken out of it called 'Judith Of Bethulia.'

"Through association with his son, I became manager of their Newark and Elizabeth Theatres. In Newark, Mr. Proctor introduced the innovation of a roof theatre playing vaudeville patterned after the American Music Hall Roof in New York. Our roof theatre was different inasmuch as the orchestra floor could be converted into a ballroom.

"He was an extremely active as well as charitable man. At his estate at Central Valley where he had a private golf links and swimming pool, I saw him at the age of about seventy, do a somersault off the spring board into the pool. He continued to retain the agility of his acrobatic youth.

"I had the pleasure of being associated with him almost twenty years. He had an extremely broad knowledge of show business, combined with great patience and vision. He was very painstaking in details and gave everyone who came in contact with him a close insight of the theatre business. He was a man of extremely high principles but very liberal in his attitude towards others. In spite of his wealth, his habits were quite frugal. The loss of his son, son-in-law and granddaughter all within a close period affected him greatly."

* * *

Lawrence J. Golde:

"Mr. Proctor was very active. He used to spend most of his nights visiting the various theatres in his circuit. Even in the latter years of his life I used to see him at the Fifth Avenue, or over in Newark, and at times up in Mount Vernon. He seldom went backstage; always was in the front of the house and chatted with his manager. He wanted his manager to take care of the theatre and gave him free rein. He never sought to butt in.

"Mr. Proctor was identified with the best in vaudeville. When you went to a Proctor theatre you knew you were going to see the best in shows.

"To my mind, Mr. Proctor, although of a very modest nature, was a very colorful character. And it was never difficult to make an appointment to see him. He always welcomed his visitors heartily. You never had to plough through several secretaries, make several appointments and stand for several postponements, as is the frequent experience of people who try to get a hearing from some modern notables."

* * *

Joseph J. Wallace, **Manager of the Grand Theatre, Albany:**

"In the twenty-four years I was employed by Mr. Proctor, I found him to be a very considerate employer. He always had a fatherly feeling towards his employes and took a personal interest in them. Mr. Proctor was one of the best showmen in the theatrical world and a business and financial man equaled by few. He reached the top of the ladder only through hard work. The theatre world will mourn his loss."

* * *

Billy B. Van:

"As I remember Mr. Proctor, he was a great showman. Having been a performer himself, I think he understood actors and could see into their hearts with the eye of his own experience. He was one of the most kind and considerate men that I ever had the pleasure of meeting in the theater. He was friendly and had the knack of making one feel at home in his presence. One thing that impressed me most and made me feel at ease was to have him call me by my first name and say, 'Well, Billy, it's nice to see you back again.'

"I have heard many so-called managers speak of actors as if they were a lot of trained animals, but not Mr. Proctor. It was always a pleasure to play in a theater under his management as you were always assured of every comfort and convenience, and under these conditions one could not help but put their heart and soul into their work. I do not know of any manager who commanded more respect than Mr. Proctor from his associates in business, with his pleasant smile and sincere appreciation of good work.

"I have often seen him when he stood in the wings or in the back of the auditorium and enjoyed a joke or a story as much or even more than the audience who had bought their ticket. He was really and truly an inspiration to many a struggling young artist.

"The beautiful theaters that he built and operated will always be a monument to his memory. I have never heard him say an unkind word to anyone. He was really and truly the father of vaudeville and lifted it to its highest level. He never allowed anyone by word or action to do or say anything on his stage that might bring a blush to the cheek of anyone in the audience. He had an understanding heart and I cherish a little poem that he once gave me which reads as follows:

> When I quit this mortal shore
> And mosey 'round the earth no more,
> Don't weep, don't sigh, don't sob,
> I may have struck a better job.
>
> Don't go and buy a large bouquet
> For which you'll find it hard to pay.
> Don't mope around and feel all blue,
> I may be better off than you.
>
> Don't tell the folks I was a saint,
> Or any old thing that I ain't.
> If you have jam like that to spread,
> Please hand it out before I'm dead.
>
> If you have roses, bless your soul,
> Just pin one in my buttonhole,
> While I'm alive and well today,
> Don't wait until I've gone away.

"I don't know whether Mr. Proctor wrote this poem or not. I often read it over and think of him with sincere respect and admiration."

* * *

Chick Yorke and Rose King:

"We worked in every theatre owned by Mr. F. F. Proctor several times during the twenties, and we had the honor of being on the bill in the last theatre built by Mr. Proctor in New York—the Proctor's 58th Street Theatre. On the opening bill were the famous Jack Benny and Mary Livingstone, and John Steel, the celebrated tenor.

"Mr. Proctor was always courteous and his word was better than any contract ever written. Every Proctor theatre always had as manager a gentleman of the finest quality. such, for instance, as Bill Quade of Proctor's Fifth Avenue Theatre."

* * *

J. Herbert Mack

"I played on the same bill with Mr. F. F. Proctor in the Bella Union Theatre, San Francisco, in either 1881 or 1882. He had just returned from Australia and did a barrel juggling act with his feet. His name at the time was Fred Levantine. He went East and I afterwards heard he acquired his first theatre in Albany."

* * *

Joe Howard:

"All actors say that Mr. Proctor was a great man, a grand fellow to talk with. He was always polite and dignified. He was a great friend of the actors. Everybody loved him very much. He had the biggest acts in show business. Whenever I had a show that made a hit, he never hesitated to give me credit for the success. He'd come back stage and say: 'Joe, that was great. Bring them to me like that all the time.' You won't find anybody who will roast Mr. Proctor."

* * *

Bill Robinson:

"I worked for Mr. Proctor in his theatres for many years and knew him personally. He was a high-type man, very considerate of other people and a great showman."

* * *

Mose Gumble:

"Mr. Proctor was the most polite theatre man I ever knew. He always had a pleasant 'How do you do,' no matter how busy he was."

* * *

Jack Norworth:

"Mr. Proctor was very reserved. He was a fine, kindly gentleman from all I could hear about him and from my personal observation."

* * *

Walter Vincent:

"I knew Mr. Proctor intimately. He was a very pleasant, soft-voiced gentleman."

* * *

Lee Shubert:

"Mr. Proctor was a man who moved slowly—which was a physical characteristic—was a good listener, not much of a talker, and seldom lost his temper."

* * *

Corinne Belle de Briou (billed as Little Corinne and Corinne, the Original):

"Mr. Proctor was a very gallant man. He was noted for his lemon-colored kid gloves, his immaculate attire and his very choice language and diction. He spoke very slowly and was always smiling. He was the most affable man I ever met. Never in all my life did I see him even the least bit ruffled. When his stage managers were frothing at the mouth, he'd be very calm, and always smiling."

* * *

A. Sayles:

"I met Mr. Proctor several times when I was on the staff of an Albany newspaper. He came to this city occasionally to look over his property. When I was a cub reporter I was assigned to go to a warehouse in this city, on the walls of which were hundreds of old show posters. The first one I saw showed a man on his back juggling barrels on his feet. The poster set forth in bold type that this was the 'sensational' Levantine act. My city editor told me that Levantine was Fred Proctor, the well-known theatrical man who started his career in Albany."

* * *

4. THE PRESS

A relative of Mr. Proctor has a scrapbook containing, among other exhibits, five editorials which honored Mr. Proctor after his death.

EDITORIAL FROM *Albany Evening News*, September 5, 1929:

Frederick F. Proctor contributed to the world's enjoyment and lightened its burden of care. He was a sort of commissioner of happiness. He might have remained for years a stage acrobat for he began his theatrical career as such but there was in his nature a strong ambition and a desire to improve himself.

He had a remarkable career. Son of a Maine physician, whose death left the family with little means, Proctor went to Boston and he found a place as a member of an acrobatic team. This team played in small theatres, later attaining some fame. With his savings Mr. Proctor, under the name of Fred Levantine, started Levantine's Novelty theatre in Green street. Albany was the scene of his early struggles. He was manager and stage hand and distributed his own bills and also acted on the stage. There were years of hardship but the young manager had determination and persistence. He formed a partnership with Henry R.

Jacobs and opened a museum at South Pearl and Beaver streets. This subsequently became a theatre and eventually he obtained control of the Leland and brought to it many famous stage folk.

In his later years he controlled theatres in many cities and became one of the most successful theatrical men in the United States.

He was known for his honesty and his kindliness and friendliness. He was one of the pioneers among modern showmen and in vaudeville. He had the gift of showmanship. He understood the tastes of the people. He had pride in his theatres and their programs, a personal interest in his extensive business. Recently he retired, selling his theatres to the Radio-Keith-Orpheum circuit. Those who knew him remember him as a real friend.

* * *

EDITORIAL FROM *Albany Times Union*, September 5, 1929:

Frederick F. Proctor was a gracious and kindly man, a public spirited citizen, a leader in theatrical activities, and he passes from life with the admiration and esteem of his fellow men. He was a notable example of a self made man, who achieved great success through his native ability, his industry and his sterling enterprise.

He was an Albanian for many years. It was here that he began his managerial career; here that he started on the highway along which he made such great progress and achieved such remarkable success. He was a native of Maine, the son of a physician, and in his youth his ability as an acrobat impelled him to enter the field of entertainment and he became a celebrity in his profession.

Mr. Proctor was the founder of a large chain of theatres and a vaudeville circuit of great magnitude. He had a deep affection for Albany and Albanians ever took a keen interest in his achievements. He was a man of broad vision and remarkable power of anticipating the amusement desires of the public, elements that contributed in large degree to his great success.

* * *

EDITORIAL FROM *Troy Times*, September 4, 1929:

The story of the life of F. F. Proctor, a remarkably successful pioneer in the promotion of chain vaudeville, who died this morning in New York after a long illness, is one of those oft-repeated American romances of rise from lowly position to that among the highest in the chosen endeavor to which he devoted his life. Starting as Fred Levantine, a boy juggler and acrobat, as one of the Levantine Brothers in the old Green Street Theatre in Albany in the days when the variety show was a rather coarse form of entertainment largely restricted to male audiences, he entered into a pioneer venture about 40 years ago by converting the old Leland Theatre in the Capital City into a vaudeville house. In his search for entertainment talent he soon branched out in the formation of a circuit and the booking of a great variety of performers, acts and the development of vaudeville features, and from this there naturally arose the demand for suitable playhouses in a chain of leading cities which would make a season's bookings a profitable venture.

His success was nothing short of phenomenal and he blazed the way in a field in which B. F. Keith and E. F. Albee became his contemporaries and later his associates in the introduction and promotion of what is popularly known as "polite vaudeville." Mr. Proctor became an important factor in raising the standards of a class of entertainment that has come to play an important part in modern life, and following an active career his demise comes shortly after turning over his interests to the new mechanical development and combination of radio, vaudeville and talking motion pictures in the ever-expanding field in which he played a leading part.

* * *

LEADING EDITORIAL FROM *Troy Morning Record*,
September 5, 1929:

DEAN OF VAUDEVILLE

While Frederick Francis Proctor, who died at his home at Larchmont yesterday, was not the originator or the "father" of the vaudeville type of entertainment he was one of the country's best known and most successful promoters of such amusement. He popularized the diversified stage programs and merited the appellation of the "dean of vaudeville." For more than fifty years he had been one of the world's most prominent figures in providing entertainment for the public.

As Mr. Proctor was born and reared in a village of Maine his early life no doubt afforded the opportunity for the observation that people liked diversified entertainment as well as the heavier productions of the stage. Commencement exercises of the district school are of this character and the entertainments of social and civic organizations are similar. In a country village they are most appreciated and best understood. As he grew into manhood and the entertainment field appealed to him Mr. Proctor readily realized the possibilities which the vaudeville form of entertainment held.

Enterprise in development as well as discrimination in selecting features for his programs characterized his career. The theatrical property which he established in Troy is a local object lesson of this policy. He built substantially, handsomely and commodiously. He made tangible returns to the communities which appreciated and patronized the entertainment he provided. As a theatre chain owner he was an extensive employer and in this capacity contributed to community welfare. Of course, in selecting features for his various vaudeville and motion picture programs he paid out large sums weekly and in this respect was a factor in the business life of the entertainment world.

In vaudeville and moving picture presentations Mr. Proctor might be considered as having held a position similar to that occupied by Barnum in the circus world and Wallack, Daly and Frohman in the dramatic field. As a builder and the owner of property he no doubt excelled any of those mentioned. Like the others in their respective lines he will be indelibly associated with the vaudeville and motion picture forms of entertainment and the millions to whom he brought amusement, almost invariably of a wholesome and inspiring character, will hold his name in pleasant remembrance.

* * *

EDITORIAL FROM *Troy Evening Record,*
September 5, 1929:

Troy feels a sense of personal loss in the death of Frederick F. Proctor. Mr. Proctor came into this city many years ago and built one of the finest vaudeville houses ever constructed in the United States. He maintained it with a type of vaudeville similar to that which he was offering to his patrons in New York and other large cities. He showed a personal interest in the affairs of the community and was a frequent visitor here.

Therefore his death, at the ripe age of 78 years, is more than the death of a theatrical king. It comes very near being the death of a successful Trojan, a man with large sums of money invested here, a man who made life in Troy happier and more metropolitan. His career reads like a romance—the Maine farm boy who, through the avenue of the showman, finally became a magnate himself. His personality was attractive and he had many friends. But Trojans will think of him in a civic way as one of themselves who achieved a lasting fame and passes into the unknown full of years and honor.

* * *

The New York World, September 5, 1929:

To F. F. Proctor America is indebted for the raising of vaudeville to a real profession, for it was his many tilts with the late B. F. Keith and other progressive managers that made the vaudeville stage a magnet for the greatest players. And it was these many battles that were responsible for salaries to individual players that far outshone those paid on the legitimate stage. In the peak of the Proctor-Keith et al. battle Americans were privileged to hear and see the cream of the profession at prices to fit every purse, for the astute vaudeville managers, even early in the game, decided that packed houses at moderate prices paid far better than half filled auditoriums at prohibitive rates. . . . Proctor, in reality, was the pioneer vaudeville manager of America. He was a born showman, although none of his family had had any connection with the stage. . . . Forming an alliance with the late Charles Frohman, Proctor two seasons later aided in forming the historic Frohman Stock Company, probably one of the greatest aggregations the American stage has known. The partnership lasted four years, but in 1893 Proctor decided the time was ripe for his program of refined vaudeville.

And it was that decision that made Proctor one of the outstanding vaudeville managers of the world. He began to build his circuit, knowing that with a chain of theatres he could offer players almost continu-

MONUMENTS TO THE MAN

ous engagement and be in position to bid for the best of them. . . . And then came his crowning feat, at least from a box office standpoint, the introduction of continuous vaudeville. With his chain complete he gave to the public all the big stars and great attractions. It is said that he could spot a player at first glance and that this intuition enabled him to lead other managers in "vaudeville finds" in which he would discover and present new talent of the finest quality.

Even when motion pictures were eschewed by other managers Proctor saw their possibilities and was the first to use them as a part of a well-balanced vaudeville bill. For more than fifty years Proctor's name was linked with all that was good in vaudeville.

* * *

FROM THE *Knickerbocker Press* OF ALBANY, January 9, 1929:

Mr. Proctor had an idea of what he wanted to do in the world; did it; tended shrewdly to his affairs and amassed a large fortune by selling amusement to the people for a fraction of a dollar, changing his form of amusement slightly as times and modes changed, but never getting far away from the idea he voiced to Charles Frohman—the idea of catering to the masses with popular-priced vaudeville entertainments.

(END OF ACT 8)

www.ingramcontent.com/pod-product-compliance
Lightning Source LLC
Chambersburg PA
CBHW031425150426
43191CB00006B/396